THE COURAGE TO ANSWER GOD'S CALL ON YOUR LIFE!

How to Live Full Out for Jesus and Be Authentically You in Christ!

Miriam Matthews

REJOICE
Essential Publishing

Miriam Matthews/Rejoice Essential Publishing
PO BOX 512
Effingham, SC 29541
www.republishing.org

Author's Website
https://define-your-dna.com/

Unless otherwise indicated, scripture is taken from the King James Version.

Scripture quotations marked (NIV) are taken from the Holy Bible, New International Version®, NIV®. Copyright © 1973, 1978, 1984, 2011 by Biblica, Inc.™ Used by permission of Zondervan. All rights reserved worldwide. www.zondervan.comThe "NIV" and "New International Version" are trademarks registered in the United States Patent and Trademark Office by Biblica, Inc.™

The Courage to Answer God's Call on Your Life!/Miriam Matthews

ISBN-13: 978-1-956775-23-5
LCCN: 2022908156

DEDICATION

I would like to dedicate this book to my loving husband, Lavar Matthews. I thank God for bringing us together. Mark 10:9 says, "What therefore God hath joined together, let no man put asunder!" It has been a blessing to share the love of God and our Union. You are an amazing father to our girls! God's love conquers all, and I am blessed that with God all things are possible! I'd also like to dedicate this book to my beautiful, intelligent, and talented daughters Zamaria and Ava. Both of you are gifts from God, and I am so blessed to be your mother! Last but certainly not least, I'd like to dedicate this book to my amazing mother, Lucy Dunson. You have been such an amazing example of what it means to be Christ-like. I appreciate your unconditional love, continuous prayers, and support! I am so blessed to be your daughter! I love you all so much!

OPENER

"Living in my Purpose feels like giving birth! A seed is being cultivated, and for that seed to grow, it necessitates a process of nurturing it and being attentive! The **labor** is the **work** that's involved to bring it forth! Oh, but when it comes forth, I have **peace**..... when I give birth! Do you want peace? Then live in your Purpose and give birth to whatever God is calling you to create!"

—Miriam Matthews

TABLE OF CONTENTS

INTRODUCTION

First off, I would like to say congratulations on purchasing this book! There are so many factors that can hold us back from living The Purpose Driven Life that God has destined for us to live. The reason why I wrote this book was due to a series of breakthroughs that I have had that allowed me to remove dark sunglasses that had been on my face for over two decades. My experience of myself, had mostly been through the lens of what I thought other people felt about me. I connected my ability to survive, to what I had to do for them, so that I could be liked. I defined my purpose by a need to fit in, while not bringing any negative attention to myself. I maintained the status quo, which created mediocrity in my life. Nevertheless, I must acknowledge that there was a fire that's burning deep inside of me that wanted to come out. This was my light, but I wasn't comfortable showing it. I felt that I had to keep it "safe," so I would blow it out at times before it could be blown out by somebody else. I vividly remembered turning 30 years old, and something changing within me. I felt like my state of being had caused so much frustration within myself, that I was going to explode, like a volcano. I went through multiple processes in God, of exposing every lie that the enemy had been telling me for years, which allowed me to begin to ground myself in the truth of who God was calling me to be. I invested in my spiritual growth and personal growth, which led me to develop mentor and mentee relationships that created accountability and elevation like Elijah and Elisha! Because of faith and works, God has created a major transformation in my life that is continuing to happen. I can no longer hide and I would be robbing the world of my purpose in God, if I chose to do so. I dare **not** commit what is **spiritually illegal** to do. I have chosen to stand in my purpose, on purpose! What I hope for you to gain from reading this book is to come to the truth and knowledge of knowing that you are the **salt and light** of the world. You will see the terms (plugging into God) throughout this book. By choosing to live for God, and remaining connected to Him, you will experience purpose and divine peace!

CHAPTER 1

PEOPLE-PLEASING BEHAVIOR

"When you're saying yes to others, make sure you're not saying 'NO' to your purpose."—Unknown

The need for belonging is an innate and instinctual part of our well-being. Even in our early childhood development, we rely on the adults around us to take care of us. Codependency, dependence on our parents or guardians to meet our basic needs, begins at an early age. During this time, we are also cultivated by cultural, family, and societal dynamics. Within the confines of these norms, we develop a framework of how to act so that we are accepted. Our need to belong is both for our emotional well-being and an integral part of our survival. Our acceptance within our families and other social systems is often maintained by how likable our behaviors are. We naturally want to preserve these solid social connections, sometimes irrespective of how the social networks' dynamics impact the framework in which we see ourselves.

For example, think of the movie Mean Girls. The group of girls has a leader, and two "subordinates," who she seemingly controls, to feed her ego. The mean leader may belittle them, call them mean names, or condescendingly speak down to them. The two "subordinate" girls prioritize their need to belong over their autonomy and view themselves. They are more interested in fitting in, therefore denying themselves their uniqueness and positive beliefs about themselves. Another way to explain why this happens is that as we grow up, we learn about ourselves by the reactions of the people around us, which translates over into how we may see ourselves and operate in other social circles. As mentioned before, our survival is based on trusting those individuals and maintaining a certain level of likability to meet our needs. Therefore this can lead to an unhealthy codependent relationship, especially since we are conditioned to assimilate.

Imagine being cultivated in a perfect environment, where our parents experienced no trauma and had no negative experiences. They only saw themselves in the way that God wanted them to see themselves. Subsequently, they had children who were also cultivated in the same way. In this narrative, no one compares themselves, everyone is confident, and this is due to their strong connection with God. Nevertheless, this family does not exist. Even when we look at the beginning of time, Adam and Eve were literally in perfection. Before Eve was in the picture, Adam was by himself. God saw that this was not good for man to be alone. God saw how detrimental it would be if Adam were by himself. Even though Adam had all of the food and animals to dominate, he was incomplete by himself. God saw the importance of togetherness and unity. Eve was God's magnificent idea. Eve was another representation of God's love, and her creation represented a purpose of togetherness and receiving/giving love. Their family unit was one. They lived in the Garden of Eden, where they had everything that they needed at their fingertips. They had a direct connection with God, and everything was perfect. However, waiting outside the Garden of Eden was the enemy waiting to steal, kill and destroy. Just think about that for a second. The enemy instantly tried his best to disrupt their connection with God by getting into their mindset. He began planting seeds of doubt concerning (who they were in God already), which created an internal discrepancy and conflict.

Even in perfection, there was a propensity to fall into the ditch of self-doubt, disbelief, and discouragement so easily. The connection between Eve and Adam was tightly connected that their decisions and actions influenced each other. Unfortunately, Adam also allowed self-doubt, disbelief, and discouragement to set in, even though (the enemy's influence) was a complete misrepresentation of Adam's purpose and how God saw him. Adam followed behind this misguided influence.

You see, our mindset or the beliefs that we have will drive our actions. Ultimately we are created to yield to God, dominate, and have a uniquely designed and divine purpose. The enemy plans to disrupt and create confusion in how we see ourselves, which can further perpetuate this disconnection between ourselves and God.

In this **perfect** environment, this still happened to Adam and Eve. Their disobedience cost them greatly. The pathology of this continued to this next generation. The mindset that their children, Cain and Abel, even led to the first murder. Cain was jealous of Abel and subsequently killed him. It's mind boggling how comparison, confusion, and lies can lead to mass chaos.

As we know, the environment in which we grow up in, is completely imperfect. We are growing up with adults facing their traumas and issues. Many adults have not addressed their traumas and have had children cultivated in immoral, conflicting, and contentious environments. The belief systems we begin to develop or (what we begin to learn about ourselves) do not represent our true selves, more often than not. These beliefs can lead us to perpetuate or recreate "this misrepresented" state of being. We are then operating in a push and pull of trying to be pleasing to others; By doing so, we create a need to constantly conform to the dynamics of the various circles we are hoping to be accepted in. This constant conformity leads to chronic fatigue, as we are disconnected from God and who we are in Him. If we're not currently experiencing a deep connection with God, peace, joy, love, and purpose, these are red flags that are telling us to get into alignment with God.

DEATH WITHOUT A FUNERAL

It is essential to recognize your current state of being. This is important because we often become desensitized to the state of our environment. Have you ever been connected to something that you didn't like but saw daily? Over time you became more accustomed to it due to the consistent and constant exposure of that environment. You did not like it per se, but maintaining that state of being created a sense of "normalcy." This concept reminds me of the children of Israel, who the Egyptians enslaved. The amount of daily labor was not something they looked forward to or liked. They were frustrated and sad. They were with their families but recognized on some level that this was not the life for which they sojourned. They wanted more! They had grown tired of pleasing the Egyptians both physically and emotionally. They began to cry out to God, who heard their cry and tried to deliver them from the hands of the Egyptians. God raised Moses to be the vessel to do His miraculous work. Moses, on the other hand, was VERY resistant to his calling. Moses had no idea who he was in God and did not think he was fit enough to be used by God. He went back and forth with God, in the most obstinate and stubborn way. After going back and forth with God, Moses stepped into his purpose. He had Aaron by his side, so that Moses didn't feel alone. God used Moses to implement seven horrific plagues on the Egyptians to emphasize that God is God alone, and to reveal God's glory. God hardened the heart of Pharaoh to be obstinate. I used to wonder why God would harden the heart of Pharaoh, instead of softening it. I realized that this is because of humanity's will to pursue ungodly things and put their pursuits before God! God said there would be no idols before Him. Humanity can be stubborn and obstinate. Therefore, this was all a part of God's plan and example to show that He is God and there is none other than Himself! This was necessary due to the disobedience and evil of the Egyptians, serving other gods and receiving "power" through evil sources. God needed to use this example to show man-crafted religions or atheists that their actions are divination to God. The obstinance and stubbornness of humankind are also mind-blogging.

One day I was listening to a documentary in which Christian historians and scientists asserted God's Word (Bible) was the original factual document of how the world came to be and was created. They felt righteous indignation and found it disconcerting that some scientists were trying to remove God from the equation with their (made up theories about monkeys/human evolution, etc. One man in the documentary said it best, "I'm in disbelief at what atheist or non-believers of Christ believe, in order to maintain their (belief) system." Yes, read that again. Under evil influences, our mindsets can lead to a disconnection from God, confusion, and mass chaos. During this time of "atheism or agnostic beliefs" and in the time of the children of Israel's deliverance, God's plan was always to also show that no matter how stubborn or obstinate people can be, His plan will prevail. God's plan was beyond what the children of Israel could even fathom.

The children of Egypt wanted to be delivered. However, they began to murmur and complain because the process of their deliverance was illusive - an unfamiliar experience that seemed to have no end. As some of the plagues took effect, Pharaoh became very hostile and increased the labor the Israelites endured. As a result, the children of Israel were discouraged and upset. **They didn't know that some things get worse, before they get better!** They began to blame Moses even though they saw the mighty hand of God and the consequences happening as a result of Pharaoh's disobedience. This "process" was unknown to them and indeed more novel than their familiar environment of slavery. At one point, they begged Moses to stop his involvement. Imagine them saying, "At least the hay for the bricks was being brought to us before you came into the picture. Now we have to get it ourselves. Because of you, our work is harder (See Exodus 5: 6-9)." Although they saw the mighty hand of God move, they allowed their discouragement and disbelief to keep them more connected to tolerating an environment that was not conducive for their divine and designed purpose. Their purpose was not to be slaves! It was to live in freedom by being obedient to God and spend the rest of their lives in a land flowing with milk and honey.

Nevertheless, keep in mind that not only had they been slaves, but they had also experienced genocide. Pharaoh ordered all of the male children being born to be murdered due to the growing population. Pharaoh felt threatened by their growth in number and wanted to break or disrupt any sense of hope or empowerment, as he did not want them to overtake the Egyptians. He wanted them to remain enslaved mentally, emotionally, and physically. Death by murder was a regular part of their environment. Nevertheless, their most basic needs (food and water) were being met. They had "houses" and knew what level of violence to expect, whether or not they had completed their marks for that day. This environment was familiar, even though it was disturbing, violent, and toxic.

Despite all this, after the process of the plagues, Pharoah yielded. They were delivered, but Pharaoh and his army pursued them. This was the cataclysmic point of God parting a massive sea so they could walk through it. Imagine a massive sea being parted right before your eyes! Imagine seeing sharks and whales in monumental proportions on each side of the sea wall. I'd be blown away with excitement thinking, " God has now created a passage for me that is entirely **UNCHARTED**. He has ordered my steps in a way that no man can do in divination, through black magic or atheism!"

Wow! This is how God works. He works in ways we can not fathom. The territory that he wants to direct us in is uncharted for us, but not for God! The new challenges and endeavors are accomplishable with him, but if we let fear stop us, we're going back to Egypt. I can say this with such confidence now, but as we can see, doubt can be so deeply rooted, especially when we're in uncharted territory and lack faith in God.

A lack of faith or belief in God, leads to complete destruction. The children of Israel watched God destroy Pharaoh and his army as they attempted to enter the sea. Why would Pharoah and his army challenge God in that way? Why would they commit suicide like that?? Again, "I'm in disbelief at the lengths atheists must go to maintain their belief system." God placed an exclamation point on the fact that He is the great "I am," "Alpha and Omega," "the beginning and the End," and "the first and last." He did more than drop the mic! He taught a massive lesson. Nevertheless, that's Pharaoh on one hand. On the other hand, even the children of Israel observing God's mighty hand, at least in 10 different undeniable ways, still had a doubt! Insane right?

We're not even talking about atheists and non-believers at this point. We're talking about the children of Israel, who were

BELIEVERS, and prayed and cried out to God to do something about their circumstances! Yet, these believers had chronic doubt ya'll! In the wilderness, they murmured and complained about everything! It was challenging for them to recognize the mighty hand of God, Jehovah Jireh, who could provide all of their needs due to God's love. It's like they had forgotten about the undeniable miracles that had just happened, which affirmed that there was more in store for them than slavery. Yet, their murmurings were deeply rooted in the familiarity of slavery, violence, and toxicity. In the eyes of God, they were utterly different from how they saw themselves. However, they began to perpetuate and recreate the murmurings and complaints that were a part of their daily function, even though God used Moses to remove them from that astronomically detrimental environment. They allowed themselves to remain mentally, emotionally, and spiritually captive to the environment that the Egyptians raised them in versus allowing themselves to experience the liberty, freedom, and provision of God.

One day in the wilderness, they even began to accost Moses. They audaciously began to express contempt about why they were being led to starving in the wilderness compared to having their most basic needs met with the Egyptians. They preferred the bare minimum as slaves just because it was familiar. The wilderness was not familiar. The uncharted territory of the wilderness was overwhelming. They let fear and anxiety of the unknown get the best of them. They had essentially normalized or become desensitized to the environment that they were in, simply due to knowing what they could expect. They were more committed to a **familiar discomfort** and unhappiness than they were to an **unfamiliar new possibility.** They had become accustomed to conforming themselves to the calamity of their environment and saw themselves through the lens of a group of people that thought they were entirely and utterly inferior. The children of Israel experienced internal conflicts with doubt, dismay, discrepancy, and discouragement. This interrupted their connection with God and their understanding of who they are in God.

It is mind-boggling how they developed a propensity to want to return to dangerous circumstances, in which they "felt a sense of belonging and met needs." This false sense of belonging commingled with their basic needs being met also cultivated their belief systems regarding how they saw themselves. They had lived in an unhealthy codependent relationship with the Egyptians for so long that they were utterly misguided about their understanding of their purpose. They developed a firm belief that their survival was contingent upon pleasing the Egyptians. They reduced themselves to the purpose that the Egyptians had facilitated or orchestrated for them. A "great" life of being beaten, murdered and fed the bare minimum. This was such a stronghold on them that they were more committed to returning than breaking off the false belief systems and being led by God's vision and plan. Acceptance of this wrong belief system was a rejection of themselves and a rejection of discovering who they are in God! Having a pulse and breathing does not constitute living the way that you are designed to by God. If you allow yourself to exist in a toxic environment, and don't take an active role in understanding who you are in God, you have not yet begun to live. As an adult, you may now take care of your own basic needs. However, if our spiritual growth and emotional intelligence have not changed with age, our emotional reasoning and fear can perpetuate the need to consent to people-pleasing behaviors and corrupt philosophy that many social circles bring. We may then allow social circles to dictate our state of being so that we're accepted by them. As long as we conform to the world or humankind, we deny ourselves growth and transformation. As long as you're depriving yourself of growth and change, you are merely existing and not thriving or living. **That is death without a funeral.**

THE COST OF COMPARISON

Why do we compare ourselves? What is the cost of comparison?

Many factors lead us to compare ourselves to other people. Often we're operating with a false sense of self in the first place. When we see other individuals living and thriving while we're just existing, it further affirms the mistaken belief about ourselves.

Sometimes we may use comparison to measure where we are, which leads us to either feel depleted or deficient. Our beliefs may tell us that we're not enough or unique enough. We may even create false narratives that specific individuals have a genetic right or innate disposition that has led to their success, which has historically been woven into the societal structure of America. Furthermore, suppose we were to even assess the complexities of being a person of color or African American in this country. In that case, we can understand that historically, our value has been completely misunderstood, and our human rights have been denied. If we were to see ourselves from the lens of oppressors or white supremacists, we would continue to per-petuate or recreate a framework of being inferior or not good enough even to try to excel. Henceforth, suppose activists such as Rosa Parks, Martin Luther King Jr., or Harriet Tubman did not see themselves through a lens of hope and possibility but fed into the rhetoric of being inferior. It's possible that we would not be as advanced as a people; although there is much progress still to be made. As long as your sense of belonging and measure of self-worth is produced by humankind, you are essentially setting yourself up to live in a state of deficiency. For some individuals, your past may have encompassed being told that you are not good enough by those who were signifi-cant. My mention of this is not to blame those individuals but to pro-vide some level of insight into why we may even trust these false be-liefs. These false beliefs will affect you even when you put your effort into creating a new lifestyle. The second something goes wrong, discouragement and dismay quickly set in and can take you off course. Have you ever heard of the saying that comparison is the envy of joy? Comparison will always be a false measure of your potential. It was disbelief and comparison in God's orchestration that led Lucifer to be kicked out of Heaven. Lucifer became so consumed with pride over his God-given splendor that he became corrupt and violent, no longer willing to serve God (Ezekiel 28:15-17; Isaiah 14:13-14). This sense of superiority led Lucifer to use his free will to scheme to be greater than God and assemble an army of angels to help him carry out that plot (Ezekiel 28:17).

It was disbelief in God's promise and comparison that led Eve and Adam to eat what was forbidden and led Cain to kill Abel. It was disbelief in God's promise and comparison that led Jacob to steal his brother's blessing and spend more than 14 years running for his life. In it all, Jacob existed in toxic and uncomfortable circumstances. I once heard a story that depicts the curse of comparison so well. It was by the late Dr. Myles Munroe, who talked about his experience on the Autobahn in Germany. The Autobahn is an area or road that has no speed limit attached to it. You can go as fast as you want to go if you so desire. Dr. Munroe spoke of experiencing an intense adrenaline rush as he was able to engage in an experience that would allow him to be liberated and go as fast as he wanted to be. He reflected on how his experiences driving in the United States were, in operating within the confines of a speed limit despite the car's capacity. This had been his experience for all of his life, until now. (The following may not be the exact numbers, but provides an illustration.) As he began to get on the Autobahn, he noticed that he wasn't driving to the car's total capacity, at 140 MPH. Instead, he moved at 90 MPH due to fear. Even though he was given permission and the right to go to the total capacity of the vehicle's speed, the commitment to the limits placed on him was more significant than his will to drive as fast as he wanted to, even with permission.

Nevertheless, he saw a car ahead of him and felt motivated to move more quickly than that vehicle. He then increased his speed to 95 mph! As soon as he passed that vehicle, he felt a sense of accomplishment. "I have arrived," he thought. He had compared his speed to the speed of a different car, and once he passed the vehicle, he felt he had made it. However, as soon as he passed that vehicle, another one zoomed by him as fast as lightning. Immediately, he felt discouraged and was in dismay. Even with him passing that one vehicle, he still hadn't gone to the capacity of his own car. He utilized comparison to critique his position, but his lack of focus on his ability didn't give him the freedom he needed to explore the car's potential or how much faster he could go. Dr. Munroe is not a professional race car driver, so trepidation is understandable. However, instead of finding the car's measure from experiencing the vehicle himself, Dr. Munroe found it in the limitations he'd been used to driving in.

Additionally, instead of trusting the experience of driving would enable growth and discovery, he compared himself and became instantly discouraged. This analogy is so amazing to me because it essentially mirrors how we operate in life. Yes, speed limits are there for a reason. It is meant to keep us safe. However, when we place this in the context of discovering potential, our previous negative beliefs can be antagonistic of our potential. I once heard that we can be more committed to safety or familiarity versus taking any risk. I'm not solely referring to dangerous situations. Our brains reminding us not to touch a hot stove is a good thing! However, our brains are also focused on protecting our ego, as much as they are focused on keeping us alive. Our ego often feels threatened, by growth or change, even if the change is beneficial. Our ego doesn't want to experience "rejection." It wants to belong in what is familiar and what it perceives as safety, which is usually camouflaged as a false sense of security. Our brains are not committed to creating inspiration and joy in our lives or even exploring the possibilities of our capacity. Many times it is more committed to safety in a way that will keep us stagnant.

Our security is often cultivated out of false beliefs about ourselves or opinions that we've been told about our capacity. We then end up recreating this throughout our lives and may create a sense of normalcy around it. If we feel it is expected, we then think it is safe. However, many of us know there's something more in us, and instead of going to our "manufacturer or creator," aka God, we compare ourselves or where we are to someone else. We do this in our families, friendships, at work, on social media, at church, and the list goes on. As a result, we're constantly misguided about where we're supposed to be. I will continuously feel deficient as long as I compare my journey to the journey of Oprah Winfrey. It is not meant for me to be the next Oprah. I intend to pray for God's will to be done in my life because His plans for me are more prominent than what I can even imagine for myself. If I constantly saw what someone else was doing and compared it to my journey, I would be utterly misguided in a way that keeps me feeling deficient, or I may feel I've "arrived," even though there's more to be done.

I'm sure you've heard of the saying, be yourself because everybody is taken. This is more than cliche. Your fingerprint is so unique that even if you had a twin, the two of you would have separate fingerprints. Every person has uniquely distinct characteristics, which only identify them. It is not meant for you to be like the next person or operate according to the limits that someone else has imposed on you unless they are by God. Nor is it meant for you to use comparison as your life's compass of where you're supposed to be.

The curse of comparison is so real. Lucifer was kicked out of heaven for it! He was in heaven, for goodness sake. What's better than that? Again, mind-boggling! His comparison cursed him to the ground. Pride and lies kept him from his purpose.

I remember when I used to think so little of myself that I would begin to have these out-of-body experiences. For example, if I felt someone else would make a particular comment that I wanted to make, I would then "approve" of my comment based on the imaginary approval of someone else. It's like I'd picture myself as another person saying a joke, or something else, which gave me a false sense of security about myself. As long as I "saw them saying it," I would then permit myself to say it. This would happen around people or in solitude, based on what I thought people would accept as cool to say. I felt safe and accepted only if I conformed to what I perceived to be acceptable to others.

The beginning of me doing this may have been sometime after experiencing sexual trauma in my childhood. Psychologists refer to it as a form of dissociation, in which I felt uncomfortable in my own body. After that experience, I distinctly remember feeling odd or off. Furthermore, some interactions with my "friends," heightened negative feelings that I had already felt about myself." More specifically, I remember being in the 4th grade and being told by a "good friend" that I was lame and annoying. I was vexed and so hurt by this experience. Why would my friend think this way about me? Because I saw her as more popular than myself and considered herself my friend, I felt that what she said about me must be true. Sadly, I didn't stop hanging around her. "She's popular, so she must be right," I thought. The opposite of right is, what? Wrong.

I began developing a sense of my identity through this experience. Imagine questioning yourself at every juncture. Am I being lame? Is this cool enough? Am I smart enough to answer this question? What will people say? This led to increasing self-doubt and diminished self-esteem. Whatever I would rehearse in my mind, I would release it in my life. After constantly rehearsing a belief that I was lame and not popular, I began to create "the false need" to be approved by others even more in my life.

I then had other experiences that I felt affirmed that I wasn't good enough. For instance, as the end of the year, (yearbook) labels were assigned at school, I remember being told that I was friendly but not popular. The popular tag was given to this other girl who everyone wanted to befriend. My need to belong was so strong that I felt instant rejection when I wasn't seen as popular. Furthermore, I remember having a crush on this boy who didn't like me but liked her. The belief that I had about not being good enough led me to confirm (the negative thought) through the different experiences. I thought, "See, I'm not good enough!" It wasn't until later that I learned, "misery loves company." Some people will try to bring you down because they don't feel good about themselves. Instead of just seeing people's subjectivity in correlation with where they are in life, meaning that people may project their own thoughts and opinions based on their own experiences. I took it to mean something negative about myself. I'd measure myself in a way that always left me feeling depleted.

Chronic comparison and conformity leads to chronic fatigue. At one point, I was afraid of relationships in general because I thought that I had to transform myself to be more likable. Based on my experiences and belief systems, my brain began to tell me it was safer to be an introvert. Living the life of a hermit or nomad became more appealing than my visibility. But in reality, even as a loner, I didn't have peace either because I'd believed the lies about myself. I denied myself any sense of hope that I could be more than a conqueror and produce greatness in this world. I was in divination with God's Word because His word says, "Greater is he, that is in us than he that is in the world (1 John 4:4)."

How dare I prioritize **doubt in myself over God's definition** of me and instruction for my life? Eureka! I was no different than the children of Israel. This is just sad. I saw myself through a lens that wasn't meant for me to see my potential. The "sad" sunglasses I would put on cultivated the method for how I created my days or interacted with others. I wanted to take those "sad" glasses off and would do so privately, but even then, I was still unsatisfied. Because I was sad on the inside, I would overcompensate on the outside. Let me say that again. Because I was miserable on the inside, I would overcompensate on the outside. I would then get on social media to continue to compare myself, and it left me feeling.......... deficient. This led me down a train wreck journey of copycat friendships, lost identity, and failed romantic relationships that created and crafted my sense of value and self-worth, which left me feeling worse than when I went into it. **Does this resonate with you? How have you compared yourself?**

UNTAPPED POTENTIAL LEADS TO CLOGGED POTENTIAL

"The wealthiest place in the world is not the gold mines of South America or the oil fields of Iraq or Iran. They are not the diamond mines of South Africa or the banks of the world. The wealthiest place on the planet is just down the road. It is the cemetery. There lie buried companies that were never started, inventions that were never made, bestselling books that were never written, and masterpieces that were never painted. In the cemetery is buried the greatest treasure of untapped potential." (Dr. Myles Munroe)

I found this so remarkable. Imagine living your entire life being consumed with thoughts of how to do everything that is pleasing to others to fit in that you never discover who you indeed are in God. This is because it requires dedication and commitment to God's assignment for you versus the social structures created by man. I remember wanting to join a sorority. To fit in and be noticed, I had to see things the way the sorority sisters saw things. Their perspective was the only one that mattered, and it "behooved me" (according to the sisterhood) to have this belief if I wanted to get in. This would have been my only ticket into acceptance. A part of this group's process was to dehumanize and condescend, which I had to accept to belong and be liked.

I just wanted to write my name.

I remember attending one of the sororities' events and standing in a long line for a long time. I was approached by different members of the organization, who would ask questions to determine my compatibility to fit in, based on the responses provided at that time. As a result of fear and anxiety, my responses were "rough and unprepared" due to my nervousness. I remember thinking, "oh my goodness, I blew it." "I'm not good enough for them."

After all the questioning, the program finally started. Before entering the doubled doors, I had to sign my name in. On a table, they provided a variety of colors of pens to write my name. I remember picking up a red pen and being verbally chastised for writing with a red pen that represented the group's color. A girl scolded me, saying, "it was not my place to write with that color pen until I was a part of a group." Uh oh, this was mean girls all over again, and I was the subordinate. I thought a pen was just a tool for writing. I didn't put any thought into their schemes to plant discouragement and doubt in me.

I just wanted to write my name but I could not do so the way I wanted. For this organization to see my worth, I would have had to pass a series of tests based on their measure. If I passed these various tests, then and only then would I have been accepted into the group. They call it the breaking down of the build-up process. Once accepted, you are part of this "amazing sisterhood." Nevertheless, I went into the room and sat through the event. After the event, a part of the process was approaching the members and engaging them. I remember coming to one girl and being told to stop talking and wait there. The feeling that I felt at that moment was dehumanizing.

People's inability to see your worth doesn't discriminate. It's a people issue.

In a country where racism is ever-present, I have not directly experienced discrimination from someone outside of my race. However, this was one of the most condescending moments by someone who looked like me and was my age. After that experience, I quickly decided that this wasn't for me. I did not want to be inducted into an organization that would only see my value if I conformed to its measure. Despite how misguided I was about my worth and subsequent "need to please," I was resistant to their process. "Oh no, she didn't," is what I wanted to say but remained quiet. Despite not going with my ego's need to fit in and please, I didn't want to shift to standing out in this way either. This was one of the few times I did not allow the rejection, pain, or opinion of circumstances to dictate how I felt about and saw myself.

Nevertheless, once the negative feelings of this experience departed from me, I wondered if I had left behind the possibility of creating a network that could advance my potential and purpose in the future. After all, that's what guided me there in the first place.....along with my inner eight-year-old's need to fit in and be cool. Nothing about this group got me or could get me closer to my purpose, from what I could see and based on my experience. It didn't appear that the mission was to get me closer to God or my divine assignment. It's not to say that these organizations don't represent a philanthropic mission. Many of these organizations end up doing great things in the community. However, we often end up plugging into the wrong network, group of friends, relationships, or media. My will to belong and have more friendships and connectedness drove me to participate in a demeaning process and not accept whatever I had to bring to the table. I let them dictate how I wrote....my...name. Isn't that ironic? I was plugged into the wrong thing.

Let's take Moses, for example. Moses was born into slavery but was delivered from it as his mother put him in a basket in a river. God's hand had been upon Moses, as God had an even bigger purpose than what he would have ever imagined. His goal was much more significant than the "perceived accomplishment" of growing up in royalty. Moses grew up with the Egyptians as if he were one. They treated him like he belonged, and he felt accepted there. Once he understood the history of his true, Israelite family, he began to face an extreme internal conflict knowing that he was a Hebrew. One day he saw an Egyptian beating the life out of a slave. His empathy for the Hebrew slaves quickly turned into anger against a particular Egyptian. This was just a typical day in the life of the Egyptian Masters and Hebrew slaves. However, Moses became "woke", attacked the Egyptian, and killed him.

Now, Moses did not think anybody saw him, and he quickly buried the Egyptian. However, unbeknownst to Moses, Hebrew slaves did see this. On a different day, Moses saw Hebrew slaves arguing with each other. As Moses began to feel more and more connected to the Hebrews, he was dismayed by their bickering and addressed it. They then rebuked him, challenging his notion of togetherness, and asked if he would kill them like he killed the Egyptian. Their murmurings about his actions, combined with fear of Pharaoh finding out about what he had done, drove him to flee and go to a different land. Moses wanted to leave every layer of identity behind him, as he felt he didn't belong anywhere.

Moses was so confused about himself, as he was seemingly rejected by both Egyptians and the Hebrew slaves. The dichotomy of his last moment in Egypt was all too overwhelming. All he could think about were the things that people said about him. He went from a prince to committing murder, to an advocate, but they saw him as a hypocrite. He wanted to use his voice and position to advocate for brotherly love, but his voice and advocacy were shut down. I don't think it's without coincidence that a part of Moses's resistance to his purpose was his emphatic belief that he could not speak in the way that God had ordered him to. Moses referenced a stuttering problem or a speech impediment that he felt would impact what God said his purpose was to do.

What do you think about that in the context of him previously speaking up and using his voice to do what he felt was right, and how it was put down even by a Hebrew slave? Moses, on some level, believed he had no place to even speak out against what was unjust. **A slave essentially told him to shut his mouth, and he susbsequently shut up his own voice.** I think he developed a framework about himself centered in the lens of what people have to say about him and his voice, and he developed anxiety and fear to use his voice. I believe he even shut it up to the point that he began to stutter! He was held captive to what they thought about him. He was confused about his identity and was plugged into the wrong opinions, even though he went in for the right intention. As long as he operated from the purview of others, his potential could have remained clogged and untapped. People can create standards for you that would never equate to the standard of God. God created Moses and his mouth like he created you and yours! When you prioritize people's opinions over God's perspective, you are giving them an authority that belongs to God. Think about it: **Who have you been giving authority to?**

The song "Barbie Girl in a Barbie World'' rings in my head.

"Made of plastic, it's fantastic. You can brush my hair, undress me everywhere. Imagination, life is your creation. Deep male voice: "Come on Barbie, let's go party!"

We are essentially living life as Barbie: other people's puppets and entertainment. We're allowing other people to be the puppeteer of what we do, how we act, and how we dress. When they say let's go party or do this or that, we consent. It seems fun at first, but we end up experiencing an identity crisis. We may realize that we have not even understood who we are and feel that our potential is clogged. You may hear people in their forties begin to murmur and complain that they feel unsatisfied and exhausted. This may seem like an exaggeration, but it is not. If you are operating according to the pulse of other people and not the heart of God, you are in divination pursuing your own purpose. Our potential and purpose are only found in our relationship and connection with God!

CHAPTER 2

SEEING YOURSELF THROUGH GOD'S MEASURE

"God's love is like an ocean; you can see its beginning but not the ending"— Rick Warren

IN THE BEGINNING

In the beginning, was the Word, and the Word was with God, and the Word was God. Everything God did in making the Heavens, Earth, and Mankind first started as a thought. When He completed everything, He saw that "it was good." He was pleased with it. God made Adam and Eve in His image and for the purpose of their maintenance of a connection with God, as they were representations of His love. He made them to love and support each other. He also made them to dominate and create! After Adam and Eve's original sin, God still had a plan for redemption. At times I have wondered why God allowed Adam and Eve to have free will. I've wondered why He didn't stop Adam or Eve from eating the forbidden fruit. I've realized that this is because of God's perfect love.

Perfect love is not about control. Perfect love grants freedom and free will. God, our Creator, certainly had the authority to prevent sin from occurring. However, love that controls is conditional. Something conditional is only present under certain circumstances. Even though there were severe consequences for their choices and sin, God continued to love them. He loved humankind so much that restoration and redemption are the essences of his unconditional and unfailing love. God created them for a purpose and understood that purpose. God gave them instruction. It was through their test and errors; they were able to understand the grave consequences of being disconnected from God. They also were able to begin understanding God's nature. This is also the first time they began to understand the threat of the enemy towards their connection with God and attack on their potential and purpose.

Nevertheless, God's grace is so sufficient that He sent His Son to pay the ultimate sacrifice by giving up His life for our sins because He loved us so much. However, that is the short end of the story. When you read through Genesis, Exodus, and even Numbers, you begin to see the method of human will and desires and the pattern of trouble that follows. Humankind has had a significant challenge with navigating "free will" when disconnected from God, especially with the constant threat of the enemy, who is the author of lies and confusion. As I mentioned before, it has been the enemy's goal since day one to steal, kill and destroy. However, God comes so that we may have life and have life more abundantly.

Jeremiah 29:11 (NIV) says, "For I know the plans that I have for you declares the Lord plans to prosper you and not harm you, plans to give you hope and a future."

Again, one of the questions that I've heard is, "If God loves me so much why do I experience pain and tragedy?" Again, perfect love equals freedom and free will. However, there are godly laws that we must follow. When we don't, we subject ourselves to consequences.

We may even be the recipient of somebody else's bad choices and disconnection from God.

Romans 8:18 (ESV) says, "For I consider that the sufferings of this present time are not worth comparing with the glory that is to be revealed to us.

However, this verse is a reminder that even though we will face trials, tribulations, pain, and discouragement, the key to coming out of it is plugging into God. God's thoughts and ways are higher than our thoughts and ways.

Isaiah 55:8-11 (NIV)
8 "For my thoughts are not your thoughts, neither are your ways my ways," declares the LORD.

9 As the heavens are higher than the earth, so are my ways higher than your ways and my thoughts than your thoughts.

10 As the rain and the snow come down from heaven, and do not return to it without watering the earth and making it bud and flourish so that it yields seed for the sower and bread for the eater,

11 So is my word that goes out from my mouth: It will not return to me empty but will accomplish what I desire and achieve the purpose for which I sent it.

These verses spell it out. It is not meant for us to remain stagnant in our connection or reconnection with God. It takes a sincere initiative for us to yield ourselves to Him, and as we do so, He will strengthen our efforts and cultivate us as we place our confidence and trust in Him. Yielding to God means seeking to understand God and His nature so that I can understand myself. Remember, we grow up learning about ourselves by the reactions of the people around us. We are around adults who are also experiencing struggles and internal conflicts.

We often have a misrepresentation of "who we are". It has always been a necessity for us to understand who we are, especially now as the loss of self is an epidemic! By understanding God's nature, I understand myself. Remember, we are made in His image. It is not meant for us to compare ourselves to anybody else. It is not meant for us to have core beliefs of not being good enough or smart enough. It is not meant for us to live in sin, which is living beneath our purpose and clogging our potential. These things happen due to trying to find purpose by pleasing our peers. However, when I plug into my Heavenly Father, I can begin to cast all of my cares or issues on Him. When I do this, I begin to experience a divine peace that the world cannot give me.

I remember feeling completely distraught to the point that I began to question the purpose of my existence. This was a dark time in my life. I constantly looked for love literally in all the wrong places. It's almost as if there was a sign that said: "**Wrong place to find love,**" and sadly, I would still go there. It's crazy to say it in that way. However, my will and desire for love, along with my disconnection from God, led me deeper and deeper into sin. Yes, I just wanted love. But instead of allowing God to restore me, I tried to handle this need in my way.

My search for love began after experiencing sexual trauma during my childhood. This was around the ages of 6 to 8 years old. Parts of me had been touched that had no business being touched. As a result of trauma, I began to have a perverted and confused understanding of my purpose. I processed everything that happened as if it were my fault. An important distinction must be made: 'This is not how I was treated or what I was told; this is how I processed it as a child'.

I carried shame for so long and I felt that something was wrong with me. I remember having multiple experiences of being disconnected from myself and being completely zoned out. (This is the dissociation that I described earlier.) I felt internally disgusting and therefore wanted to constantly escape through daydreams mentally.

As I grew older, I felt that my body wasn't truly mine because of the negative core beliefs that I had developed. This was coupled with wanting to give my body away because I didn't want the images of my childhood sexual trauma in my head. I, repeatedly, tried to empower myself in the wrong way. Every time I did this, I would expect a good result. However, each man continued to disappoint me to the point that I felt all men were the same. Ironically, I didn't see how I was creating insanity in my own life. What is insanity? Doing the same thing and expecting what? A different result. Because the measure of my purpose was misrepresented, I began to misrepresent my purpose. I didn't learn how to allow God to truly heal my pain. While trying to "empower" myself, I perpetuated my pain. The bad thing is, I didn't see how I was repeatedly recreating my trauma.

Every time I began new relationships, I would have a rejuvenated hope that things would work out. When they did not work out, I would be utterly dismayed. I did not take disappointment well at all. Instead of reflecting on why things had gone wrong, I would rationalize each of the relationships or break-ups as meaning that I wasn't good enough.

I did feel I was worthy of love. However, I didn't have a good understanding of what love was in the first place. For me, love began to mean the toleration of bad behavior without consequences. When I was actively living in these patterns, I did not understand this was my definition of love explicitly. Because I saw myself through a distorted lens, my standards deteriorated, and the bar or my expectations for a loving relationship became lowered significantly. I couldn't understand why I couldn't replicate or experience the love I saw in the cartoon movies that I'd watched in my childhood, such as Cinderella, Aladdin, Snow White, etc. As silly as it sounds, this was all I wanted. I was a fiend for love.

I truly wanted to be loved and accepted, and I sought it out so hard. Now I understand that it was because I just really wanted to love and accept myself.

I remember meeting the man of my dreams. I was in love, but kept my past to myself. I was ashamed. Conviction struck me and I realized I needed to open up and be transparent with him. This was a major disruption in our relationship. As I revealed my past to him, I felt the backlash of shock and despair from him and those connected to him. I remembered being told that "my dynamics" are not a good fit for him.

You see, I had a child before him during my search for love. Additionally, I was coping with the heartache of becoming disjointed with my church home. I had been attending this church for my entire life. "I was seen as an ideal child and young adult until I could no longer hide the evidence that showed I was not: my child." "Little Mimi," they would call me, wasn't little and innocent anymore. Poster children aren't supposed to sin or get pregnant. They hadn't known about the pain of my trauma, but I felt the judgment about the presence of my pregnancy. However, I think they were actually more shocked than judgmental because I made it look like my life was perfect, and hadn't dealt with the pain and loneliness that I felt on the inside that came as a result of trauma. **I had pain in private, and pride in public**, which led me to be "what everyone needed" and further perpetuated my people-pleasing behavior. I felt like I didn't fit in anywhere. Complete loss of identity, and God needed to take the blinders off my eyes. His (the love of my life), response to the transparency of my past wasn't his fault. I shouldn't have kept it from him and did that because of the shame I had been carrying. **Colossians 3:9-10** says, "Lie not one to another, seeing that ye have put off the old man with his deeds; and have put on the new man, which is renewed in knowledge after the image of him that created him."

God didn't want me to feel this way or live like this any longer. God wants us to live in integrity and truth! Remember: "Ye shall know the know the truth, and the truth shall set you free?" There's freedom in truth! I believe God used this experience, or this moment in which I felt so deep in the ditch and disconnected from literally everyone so that I could focus solely on Him! I felt so completely disconnected that I **finally** picked up my Bible. I didn't know where to start. I had stopped going to my home church and sporadically attended other churches. I didn't remember the last time I read my Bible. I felt I had nothing to lose by picking a random Scripture to read. I had done this before, but this time was different.

Romans 8:1 appeared before me. **There is therefore now no condemnation to them which are in Christ Jesus, who walk not after the flesh, but after the Spirit.**

I could have opened the Bible, and any other Scripture could have appeared before me; however, this was the page that opened. This was the Scripture that my eyes immediately landed on. The divine peace that I felt at that moment was indescribable. God's Word says I will give you peace that surpasses your understanding. When I tell you, this was the first time I truly understood that verse, and I felt a divine peace beyond what I could fathom. I mean it.

This peace felt so comforting and safe. This peace made me cry tears of joy instead of tears of sorrow. This peace was healing and covered my pain. It began to help me reframe my thinking and affirm that I am loved by the one whose love is perfect! I began to experience something divine (right in my own bedroom). That helped me to begin a journey of healing. Seeing yourself through the eyes of people will perpetuate pain. However, plugging into God will heal your pain and empower you to see yourself as who He designed you to be. Even in my trauma and disconnection, God's love was sufficient, powerfully redemptive, and met me right where I needed him to meet me. My previous emotionally painful state wouldn't have sustained or fostered a healthy relationship. It seems that falling into a ditch completely was what I needed to stop making the "wrong turns due to carrying shame." In the ditch, all I could do was plug into God! **Do you remember looking for love in the wrong place or experiencing a poor outcome in a relationship because you weren't ready for the healthy sustainability of it? How does Romans 8:1 resonate with you? What do you want God to heal in your life?**

"GOD IS NO RESPECTER OF PERSONS."

As an African American woman, my journey to understanding my value has had significant complications. This is especially so compounded with the historical context of society's thoughts about people of color. My ancestors were sold into slavery and were slaughtered, raped, held captive, and demeaned for hundreds of years. It is mind-boggling that this institution was constitutional at some point. God never meant for humankind to physically and emotionally abuse and enslave each other. That was very clear in Genesis.

God instructed mankind to rule over the animals and grounds, not people. However, remember that humanity perverted free will. One-way humanity has perverted its will is by making its view superior to God's law. The children of Israel, like my ancestors, were also sick and tired of being slaughtered and abused physically and emotionally. They were tired of being treated as inferior, even though their blood would bleed the same color as a Caucasian person in this country. Just as the Egyptians enslaved and slaughtered the children of Israel who contributed to the growth of Egyptian society, Africans and African Americans were also exploited.

People of color have historically been oppressed and denied basic human rights, including the rights to education, healthcare, and voting, to name a few. In fighting for their rights, they were placed in prison. They were sprayed with water hoses as if they were animals. Some animals were treated better than black people. Black people saw this and were traumatized. I was traumatized by learning about the consequences of fighting for one's rights. It is traumatizing to see your fellow peers murdered right in front of you or on television.

In history class, I recall learning about the emancipation from slavery and the Jim Crow Era ideals of separate but equal. I also remember learning about the African-American child Ruby Bridges, whose parents wanted her to have a better education. She was taken to an all-white School during which she was being yelled and cursed at, and spit on by white parents who did not want her at their school. I can't imagine how she may have felt. She was a child. Children, teenagers, and adults (humans) need to feel safe. However, she was the direct recipient of hatred solely due to the color of her skin. Learning about my history didn't leave me feeling empowered. I felt sad about what had transpired. Prior to President Obama being elected, I felt it didn't even seem possible to have a person of color in that position. It felt like doom and gloom, as people with my skin color's value had been misrepresented for hundreds of years. This was an external part of my upbringing and a reality that I constantly faced.

We did not spend a lot of time talking about the contributions of African-Americans. African Americans were not recognized for their intelligence, but rather their physical strength or physical exertion. In this post-slavery society, racism has continued. I must admit that it had previously been one of my most difficult challenges to see myself in a positive light.

Colorism was also ever-present in my community. "The lighter, the better." **It's amazingly sad how we can believe that lie.** I remember thinking my skin color wasn't good enough. It's sad to think about how melanin, which is simply produced as a means of protection from the sun and a result of being closer to the equator was used as a weapon that even impacted the mindsets of those who are oppressed by it. There seemed to be an epidemic of purchasing creams to lighten up skin tone. This was done among African Americans to create a European style of beauty, but it really shows the extent of mental slavery in this post-slavery society.

One of my greatest challenges was when my family and I moved to Massachusetts. I experienced a major culture shock. Where I lived before was largely around people of color. In Massachusetts, we lived in the city of Framingham and then Ashland (majority Caucasian), and I worked in the cities of Chestnut Hill and Needham. I worked with a majority of the leadership and those people were Caucasian as well. I remember starting my first day as a social worker in the Skilled Nursing Facility and being amongst the leadership team. The nurses and certified nursing assistants were majority Haitian-American/people of color. I remember one of the nurses looking at me in shock and in disbelief. At first, I did not understand it, but later on, I understood. They hadn't seen a person of color, such as myself, in that position before. All of the social workers before me were Caucasian. I wasn't confronted with any explicit issues surrounding racial tensions. However, I began to give even more thought to my skin color.

As God was blessing us, we wanted to buy our first home. We went to different open houses but did not see anyone that looked like us. My skin color was constantly on my mind like a gnat that would not fly away. I constantly wondered what people thought of it, and this also made me insecure. Fortunately, we found a house, which was a difficult feat as the houses in the area went fast. We moved in and nervously met our neighbors. They were actually nice! I felt lucky but mentally scattered due to the constant looming feelings of inferiority and paranoia. I felt that I was being watched every time I would leave my house. Talk about high levels of stress! It is hard to describe the feeling behind constantly thinking about your skin color and fitting in at a job where you are not largely represented amongst the leadership.

It's hard to describe the feeling of thinking you are being scrutinized because of your skin color, even as you're walking down an aisle in the grocery store. Breaking free from this required standing on truth, and mentally reframing. This would enable me to break free from the mental bondage! God's Word says that He is no respecter of persons. He rains on the just as well as the unjust. God doesn't call us according to our purpose based on the shade of skin. God looks at our hearts and not our demographics. We may look at the circumstances surrounding ourselves and wonder if there is any hope beyond what we can see. However, God sees beyond what we can see, and will place a passion in our hearts; that if we yield to it, we will no longer be held captive to the circumstance. If Harriet Tubman did not see beyond the existence of slavery, many would not have been saved from its cruelty. If Martin Luther King Jr. did not see beyond the circumstances, his dream would only be a dream.

Sometimes people may feel that the mistakes they've made in the past have cut them off from being used by God. God will use any vessel willing to be used. Look at the example of the Apostle Paul, a Christian killer, and unbeliever. Who would have thought that he would become a radical believer in Jesus? However, he yielded to

God and became radical about the redemption of sinners. God used him in a very mighty way.

As a matter of fact, he ended up writing many books of the Bible. To think that a person who once chastised and slaughtered Christians could also be redeemed and radicalized about Jesus Christ. Then he would subsequently write multiple books of the Bible is beyond what we can fathom! Imagine what God could do in your life if you yield to Him! Many of the barriers we have are based on our own perception. Well, perception can be deception! Remove your "perceived barriers," which create blindness leading you to get off course. When we yield to God, He covers all of our sins. He doesn't see anyone as better than the other. God doesn't have favoritism. He will use you if you're willing to be used. The key is to be willing. You must be willing to not see your value from the historical context of what has happened or the present circumstances surrounding you. The key to being used by God is plugging into Him, so you can answer His call! Do this so He can give you wisdom, knowledge, and understanding that will lead you on a path towards fulfilling your purpose.

IF GOD CAN USE A DONKEY, HE CAN USE ME.

I am absolutely not demoting our value to that of an animal; however, this story amazes me when I read it in the Bible! As we know, the children of Israel were on their journey in pursuit of God's promises to them. Balak was a Moabite, who felt threatened by them, and knew that his kingdom would eventually fall due to evil and idolatry. He wanted Balaam (a prophet) to curse the children of Israel, and offered Balaam riches/gold, etc. He couldn't understand the value of the children of Israel, but how could he? He didn't worship God, nor did he yield to God. This lets me know that humankind can come up with distorted reasons that will perpetuate inferiority, jealousy, comparison, envy, leading to murder, hatred of others, and ultimate destruction. Balaam didn't want to respond but felt pressured. He asked God if he should go, and God disapproved. He ended up getting on the road, and while riding his donkey he was blocked by an angel of God. The donkey stopped moving, but Balaam was unsure of the reason it stopped. Balaam assumed that the donkey was being stubborn. He was unable to see the angel that the donkey could see. Therefore, anytime he would hit the donkey to go, the donkey would hit a wall. This caused Balaam to injure his foot.

Balaam hit the donkey three times out of immense frustration when God opened the donkey's mouth to talk. "Why are you hitting me? I have not done anything to do," said the donkey. A donkey spoke words! Wow. Balaam was so blinded by the extremity of this situation that he became distracted. Balak (a very rich, entitled king) wanted Balaam to change his stance so that God's children would fail; however, God's plan prevailed and will always prevail even if we can not see it. Just look at the beauty of this contrast: A rich, entitled king could not have his way, BUT God used a DONKEY to further His plan and message! **If God can use a donkey to speak the truth, then we can utilize the truth to expose EVERY LIE!** Come on church, can I get an amen?! It doesn't matter what scheme society will come up with to make you feel inferior, or lead you to feel that you're missing out. Stand on the truth of God's promises and your identity in God!

ARE YOU AN A.L.I.E.N?

What on earth does this mean, Miriam? Anointed, Leader, Intelligent, Empowered, and Non-conformist! I'm a proud A.L.I.E.N! God's Word tells us not to be conformed to this world but be transformed by the renewing of our minds. God is telling us this as a warning for our protection. Imagine constantly feeling the need to fit in no matter the consequences. Whoever I surround myself with, I will become. Have you ever heard of the saying birds of the same feather flock together? I've also heard this stated differently. Let me know your top five friends, and I will understand who you are. When I am determined to fit into the crowd or certain social groups, I deny myself, my own unique identity and purpose in God. When we do this, we are more inclined to take on the shared identity and experiences of the groups we're in. We must be cautious of fitting in, for the sake of fitting in, to the detriment of being authentically ourselves.

Do you only feel "yourself" when you are at home? I remember feeling this way constantly growing up in my teenage years. I had essentially forgotten how to be me in public. I didn't feel it was safe to be me. I felt that my emotional survival was dependent upon assimilating. I would constantly assimilate to the point that there were variations of me for each environment I entered. There was one version of me at work, at church, at home, or anywhere else I would find myself. Many times this would drive me to the point of exhaustion. At first, I thought that this was due to my personality being more introverted than extroverted. However, this had less to do with my personality and more to do with the negative core beliefs I upheld within. I tried to acclimate to various environments and in the process forgot how to be myself.

Nevertheless, God's Word is saying that conforming yourself to the ways of this world, especially in the context of perversion and sin, will automatically get you off course. You risk losing connection with God. To conform is to change yourself in a way that makes you fit in with something else. If God is not influencing me, I am likely being influenced by something else.

WHAT ARE YOU BEING INFLUENCED BY?

Many of the things that we've become influenced by or the individuals we're trying to be like in the world, have to do with the lust of the flesh. We are constantly in a battle between spirit and flesh. The only way for our flesh to be controlled is by allowing God's Spirit to be greater than our fleshly desires. However, if we're not plugged into God, we are led by our fleshly desires, or the fleshly desires of others may also lead us. Furthermore, whatever I am plugged into will shape me. Think of how an item, such as a lamp is plugged into the wall. Its source is the energy, which "feeds it" to turn on. Just like that, we're fed by everything we plug into. We may plug into different things such as television: reality shows that depict constant drama and fighting, drugs and alcohol, partying and drugs, derogatory music, sexually perverted movies, and immoral books, etc.

I hear someone saying, "well goodness, can't I live? Can't I relax and be entertained?" **Well, whatever you plug into will influence you and while you're "entertaining yourself," you don't want to end up being the enemy's entertainment!** The places you go, the books you read, and the people you meet all have some impact or influence. Suppose you're constantly surrounding yourself with the wrong things that are divination to God. In that case, over time, this can lead to being desensitized to evil. Do you think evil is a strong word to describe a reality show or social media? Have you ever left social media and felt noticeably worse after leaving that space? Why didn't you feel better about yourself? Why didn't you feel empowered after watching all of the drama and conflict on the show to be authentically you and step into God's purpose? All of these forms of entertainment or things plant self-doubt, discouragement, distraction, denial, and delay in your life. If you're not constantly engaging in a community or material that is godly and for your spiritual and personal growth, then you are wasting your time, and your potential will be clogged within you. The more you watch the drama play out on shows or social media, the more garbage you consume.

Whatever you rehearse in your mind is what you will release in your life. Let me say that again, whatever you rehearse in your mind is what you will release in your life. Once upon a time, I asked someone what they would have for dinner tonight. They said, "Maybe a steak, some potatoes, and a vegetable." I said, "Great, now will you go and get your ingredients from the garbage?" They said, "Of course not!" When I asked them why, they said that it was gross and unsanitary. It would ruin their dining experience and likely cause them food poisoning. I said exactly! However, they couldn't understand why their daily experience was full of chaos and confusion. They had been "fed" with mental garbage! For you to change the future, you must change what you focus on today. If you wouldn't make your meal tonight with yesterday's garbage, then stop making today's experiences or tomorrow's experiences with the garbage you have been plugging into or the mental garbage from decades ago. **Whatever you surround yourself with is what you will release in your life.**

I remember wanting to "fit in." I would watch the reality shows and talk about them with my social circle. I wanted to blend in so much that I'd go to parties, drink alcohol and throw my body around. I made myself into a replica of others instead of being the original version of me. However, I learned that one of the keys to understanding my purpose is realizing that I am meant to be peculiar. **We are peculiar treasures.**

Exodus 19:5 says, "Now, if ye will obey my voice indeed and keep my covenant, then ye shall be a peculiar treasure unto me above all people: for all the earth is mine."

Therefore, understanding who I am requires that I be unique and different. If I am focused on my unique purpose, the light that God has given me will become radiantly bright. The more I assimilate, the more I am turning my light off and dimming my light. My sisters and brothers, you are a unique lighthouse. I once heard that a lighthouse is a lighthouse whether boats are in the ocean or not. We are often waiting on boats or people to validate us in a way that gives us purpose or permission to turn our lights on. However, God's Word says you are the salt and light of the earth!

Furthermore, you are fearfully and wonderfully made! The purpose that God has instilled in you is what He wants to bring out all of you. However, to do this, realize your permission comes from God, just as your value already came from God. When you conform to God's ways and place your confidence in Him, this allows you to cultivate the spiritual aptitude to overcome your flesh and the negative opinions of others. God will develop you in a way that you are solely focused on His divine peace. He will empower you to persevere despite any attack from people or principalities. The more you try to be like someone else or the group of people that you want to fit in with, the more you become a stranger to yourself. I no longer knew myself. I've worked with so many clients who are much older that stated they don't know their God-given identity. Well, when you've spent your life being something you're not to please other people, **you become a stranger to yourself.** But when you realize and recognize that you are a stranger in this world and are meant to STAND OUT, you can then stand on the truth of knowing that you are NOT a stranger to God. You are a child of God.

In knowing that you are a child of God, your identity is found in Him. No more identity loss! Knowing who you are and whose you are, gives you the confidence and permission to focus on the mission at hand. No one on this earth will understand me as God understands me. Do not conform to this world. Conform to God. Be a stranger to this world but know who you are in God. This is essential to unlocking divine peace and a unique purpose.

MIND TRANSFORMATION

2 Corinthians 5:17 (NIV) says, "Therefore, if anyone is in Christ, the new creation has come: The old has gone, the new is here!"

Be more committed to who you are becoming in God than who you were familiar with. This was a fantastic concept and quote that I heard from a great orator discussing human behavior. Many times, after we accept God as our Lord and Savior, the battle with our flesh continues. Nevertheless, it is essential for you only to see who you are in Christ and stand on that truth. There are individuals who may have known you before you became saved by God's grace and accepted His salvation. They were privy to 2% of information about you, yet think that they know 100% about you. However, they do not know who you are in Christ.

Furthermore, it is not up to you to convince them about who you are in Christ. Sometimes we become frustrated even when our church family does not understand who we are in Christ. We often feel that we are being mistreated and judged. It is your responsibility to plug into God and allow him to continue cultivating you, which will enable you to grow. God wants to develop you in a way that enlarges your capacity. When your capacity changes and is enlarged, you're able to operate in the timing of God and answer His call.

Remember, God plans to restore and redeem His people. It was always His plan to save and restore you. Many times we do not quickly cease trying to find validation through people. However, you must remain constant in your relationship with God. God wants to give you new revelations and insights daily. God wants you to renew your mind and pray daily. Being a new creature in Him requires a new lifestyle. The old things are passed away, which also means forming godly habits and releasing old habits. How do I stop being a habitual sinner?

The answer to this is to give it to God, pray and activate faith. We make this harder than it has to be. When we begin to prioritize the will of God in our lives over our own will, we are positioning ourselves to resist temptation and form new precedents in our lives. Yes, this is a new journey and a process. However, remember God is Master Potter, and you are the clay. God wants to shape and form you as you constantly yield to Him. Praying without ceasing isn't a joke in this process of being a new creature. The lesson of Adam and Eve in the Garden of Eden teaches us that being anointed comes with attacks. You must always remain prayerful about aligning new behaviors with a purpose that God has instilled in you.

Being prayerful helps you to stand on guard and protect your purpose. Greater is He that is in you, than He that is in the world! When you plug into God, you will be able to persevere no matter what and have a victory-based mindset. God's Word says that tribulation worketh patience. As you are a new creature, God will take you through a process that will help you develop the patience to work with and hear from God. Patience in the process is necessary for the preparation for your calling. Sometimes we think that because we are new creatures in God, things should happen instantaneously. However, God wants to cultivate us so that we will be able to handle the elevation that He provides. For example, if I mismanage $100, I will likely mismanage $1,000. The Word says do not despise small beginnings. God wants you to become a good steward of everything that He gives you, but this begins with developing your relationship with Him and remaining committed to the process!

CHAPTER 3

FORGIVENESS

HALL OF HATERS

"You can not go through the door of DESTINY without passing through the hall of haters."—TD Jakes

Again, being anointed comes with attacks because the enemy does not want you to succeed. Jesus, who did not sin and spoke no evil, was hated by many! Jesus was about His Father's business from a very young age. He knew that he had the assignment to fulfill and did not want anything to deter him from that assignment. Once Mary and Joseph were looking for Jesus, who was young at the time. They thought they had lost him and became very frantic when they searched for Him and could not find Him. As a parent, this is completely understandable. Nevertheless, later they found that he was in the temple, studying and learning. The Word of God says to study and show yourself approved, which is what He was doing. He was preparing for His assignment.

After all, plugging into God by understanding His Word is key to fulfilling your divine assignment. I think this story is so amazing because they didn't find Him playing outside. They found Him studying. I'm sure there were times that He did play and had fun. Yet, He knew He was different at a young age. When they found Him, Jesus' response was, "Did you not know that I'm about my Father's business?" Even at His age, Jesus didn't allow the perception of others or their expectations of Him to deter Him from deepening His relationship with God. Jesus made up His mind that His purpose would far exceed His need to please people, including His parents.

Of course, Jesus understood why they were looking for Him, and it's understandable why they would become frantic. They knew that their child was the Son of God, a redeemer for all. But as parents, they wanted to keep Him safe. I can imagine that there were other times that they may have felt a disturbing feeling about Jesus's actions because of all the unfamiliar experiences anticipated to happen because of His supernatural birth and purpose.

They didn't know it all, and not knowing it all can be overwhelming inspite of prior confirmation and prophecies. For example, an angel visited them during Mary's and Joseph's courtship. Mary gave birth to Jesus as a virgin. Three wise men visited them. Anna, a prophet, whom they didn't know, randomly confirmed that He was the ultimate redeemer. Ultimately, this example serves as a reminder that even those close to us may have difficulty understanding our purpose and our passion at times.

How do we handle people's shortcomings and misunderstandings of us?

At times I have wondered why Jesus turned water into wine. "My time has not yet come," Jesus told his mother. Here's the backstory: they had a gathering, and they ran out of wine. Mary then asked Jesus to turn the water into wine. I wondered why Mary would have desired for Jesus to use His supernatural powers to make more wine for the gathering. He instructed the servants to fill the jars with water and turn it into wine. He did it! Jesus made this happen, as He understood that Mary was thinking from **her own perspective and capacity.** Jesus didn't put her down because she lacked awareness about the proper timing or that she had mistaken her expectations of Him and what He should be doing. Even in this example, Jesus prioritized **keeping His heart open through honor and compassion, through which God's glory was revealed.** The Word says to live peaceably with all men if possible. Jesus could have gotten upset and disappointed with His mother but chose honor instead. Many times we become frustrated with those that are closest to us, because they may fall short of the expectations we place on them. I believe that God understands that we all have different perspectives and are in different places in our journey of being Christ-like.

CHARITY BEGINS AT HOME

This phrase is something my mom would constantly say. I understand it now more than ever. Many times we feel our families have the most dysfunctional dynamic. However, the dysfunction of our families' behaviors provides us a major opportunity to learn patience, conflict resolution, and peace, which can create uniformity within our family. If you can do this in your family, you can do this in other places, which better equips you to stand strong against spiritual warfare and situations that drive disconnection and chaos! Jesus was able to do this by creating a strong foundation, which prepared Him for attacks.

THERE'S SOMETHING ABOUT AGE 30

Jesus's ministry began at the age of 30. He did a 40 day and 40 night fast, which ignited His ministry. He separated Himself from everyone including His own family. This was necessary to align Himself with His purpose. Sometimes elevation necessitates and requires separation. Imagine fasting for 40 days and 40 nights and only drinking water. Imagine being in the desert or wilderness by yourself to connect to God and receive clarity about your purpose. The enemy did not like this.

As Jesus was ending His fast, He was tempted by Satan himself. Satan wanted Him to prove His power. Satan challenged His ego instead of focusing on God's timing and instruction. Many times we are led by our ego because our focus is on pleasing the people around us. Or maybe we want to prove them wrong because they said that we wouldn't be anything. Therefore, our actions are motivated by the wrong people or the wrong thing. This doesn't bring peace because the wrong motivation is at the root. **The temporary satisfaction of the ego is never worth the long-term experience of God's peace.** When our actions are motivated by God, God's glory will be revealed in us. As a result, people will be saved and lean closer to God.

However, the example of Jesus being tempted also shows that not everyone is for you. The potential is always there for others to tempt you by disrupting your connection with God. Being led to please others is also agreeing to be led by your flesh and principalities. The consequence of this can lead to discouragement, doubt, denial, and delay. One of the major issues with this is that people are not God. They could be with you one minute, and the next minute they are not.

God is the same yesterday, today, and forever. God is not a man who should lie, and only He knows what He has planned for you. Only He knows your purpose. Pride and ego lead us into pleasing others to receive instant gratification. However, God cultivates our confidence in a way that allows us to develop patience and experience peace. Pleasing people leads to fatigue, a false sense of self, division, and pain. **Pleasing God** leads to peace, truth, wisdom, knowledge, understanding, and resilience. "How did Jesus beginning His ministry with a fast, help Him with forgiveness and focus? In the context of forgiveness, a key aspect of it is humility. The other perspective is that Jesus's fast, helped Him to stay humble versus being led by pride. During this fast, Jesus humbled himself, allowing him to have discernment and clarity to see the principality and temptation. In being able to see with OPEN spiritual eyes, what/who we're dealing with and their motives, we can better protect our HEART and PURPOSE by resisting the plots of the enemy. In other words, humbling myself before God allows for wisdom and understanding. If I can discern the enemy operating behind people, I'm more apt to steer away from troubles, pray, and guard my heart which keeps me on course! One of my mentors says, "When people are acting up, you know there's a spirit behind it, therefore why reduce yourself to a demon by responding the same way they are acting?" God gave us tools to protect ourselves the right way, which I'll discuss in-depth later. Ego and pride can create situations for us to have more issues! Humility under God, activates COURAGE, LOVE, and DISCERNMENT, leading to more peace!" **Which one is more sustainable over the long term? How?**

FORGIVE FOR FREEDOM

The reason God cares about your heart is that He wants you to be in touch with Him, which allows your heart to remain open for possibilities. The Scripture says to guard your heart because out of it flows the issues of life. If I allow resentment, anger, or any negative emotion to take up space in my life then I am limiting my capacity to be open to the new experiences or purposes that God has planned for me. Essentially, I will be more focused on preserving my life instead of experiencing something new. The more I do this, I am existing and not living. I would be making an agreement within myself that people's opinions are more important than my peace and purpose.

This is not a way to live. This is what the enemy wants. The enemy wants you to feel unloved and will tell you lies about yourself. The enemy will also use the people closest to you and strangers to plant lies, discouragement, doubt, and any scheme to keep you from tapping into your potential. He doesn't even want you to realize that you have potential and purpose. Forgiveness is essentially opening up your heart's capacity to live in your purpose. Not forgiving is agreeing with being a prisoner to your emotions.

WHY DOES FORGIVENESS SEEM HARD?

People do not often want to forgive because it feels like condoning the offensive behavior. However, this is not true. Jesus asks us to forgive, so our heavenly Father will also forgive us, and so our hearts can be open for receiving and giving love going forward. If even 2% of resentment is held within our bodies, this is 2% less of our hearts capacity that we are not using. Essentially, no one is perfect. Imagine not recognizing this as an adult, and personalizing every negative interaction that is experienced with other people. Internalizing the pain from the experiences of others mistreating you is also consciously and subconsciously agreeing that their action is an indication of your identity. The following story explains this example. One woman had experienced emotional trauma in her childhood and teenage years by a parental figure. She had a few friendships, but these friendships were fickle. She truly desired companionship but had grown to either perpetuate unhealthy relationships or cut people off so quickly due to the fear of being hurt. She lived on these two extremes.

RELEASE THOSE BAGS

In some of the relationships she had, it was challenging to set healthy boundaries and address offenses out of fear of losing the relationship. She then maintained toxic relationships, which would create and perpetuate unhealthy codependency. Although she was aware of this, it was challenging for her to want to communicate or implement healthy boundaries because, at some level, she accepted that this was better than nothing.

1.Mag. "Release Those Bags: A Picture Which Says It All..." MAG's Blog, October 15, 2016. https://marieabanga.wordpress.com/2016/10/16/release-those-bags-a-picture-which-says-it-all/.

Furthermore, it was difficult for her to develop new healthy relationships as she felt this would be too much work and exhausting. Forgiveness was the issue. Forgiveness created and exacerbated fear, which emotionally stifled her. She had been carrying around the emotional luggage stemming from her childhood, leading her to recreate painful relationships in her adult life.

The emotional intelligence that she has now with her relationships is connected to the emotional pain of her experiences in her childhood and teenage years. **We can age, but our emotional intelligence can be that of a 7-year-old.** She understands forgiveness but has chosen not to forgive. It has been years since she has spoken with her parental figures. Again, the lack of forgiveness, can be described as (maintaining a certain position due to the fear of being hurt again.) Fear doesn't allow for the growth of discernment or clarity. By maintaining her pain to protect herself from those who hurt her in her childhood, the maintained pain is causing pain in future relationships. The woman truly wants to experience love and compassion. However, her potential is being clogged, as she is being consumed by the past, which is taking up space in her present. She experiences negative rehearsed thoughts about herself that are tied to the past painful experiences. This leads her to feel discouraged despite not being in contact with her family.

The second extreme encompasses quickly cutting people off without addressing issues as they arise. She then internalizes more pain experiencing loneliness when her deepest desire is companionship. On some level, it appears that she has agreed with a negative core belief of being unlovable and unable to maintain or have healthy relationships due to the previous actions of her parental figures. Her decision not to forgive keeps her from (growing emotionally) even though she's aging physically. Not releasing the pain has also created insanity, as she is doing the same thing and expecting a different result. She now suffers from multiple mental health disorders, including anxiety and depression. Her depression manifests as a continual fostering of her hurt about what has happened in the past and anxiety is caused by being worried about the hurt that may happen in the future. **Forgiveness in the context of healthy boundaries** allows you to address issues proactively and as they arise, so that the relationships in your life are actually meaningful relationships. Forgiveness helps you maintain forward momentum and opens you up to new possibilities. **Are you struggling with forgiveness? How do you think the lack of forgiveness is impacting you?**

LET THAT SOFA GO!

Learning how to manage your emotions is important to maintaining forward momentum. Experiencing tribulations are inevitable to being a human on earth. As imperfect people constantly surround us, we will experience pain, disappointment, and trauma at some point or another. Nevertheless, we are also made to experience emotions. We are not robots. God created us to be multi-dimensional in that way. It is with our emotions that we can experience His joy. It is with our emotions that we can experience empathy and care. For example, we can see an unjust situation or circumstance and do something about it. Having emotions is a good thing. It would be concerning if you did not have emotion. Not having emotion is also referred to as being a psychopath. Not being able to feel or understand the emotions of others keeps us distant and not relatable. If we learn how to connect with our emotions and manage them, we grow emotionally and our relationships benefit.

I heard of this helpful analogy once. Imagine having a sofa that represents every negative emotion that you can think of. The sofa has been with you for years, and it has all types of tears in it. Cotton is falling out of it because the tears have gotten so big. This sofa represents the traumatic experiences that you've endured in your childhood, teenage years, or adult years. This sofa has also represented the **familiar** negative emotions so that you can keep them. It is a constant reminder of why you are not good enough and why it's not meant for you to have healthy relationships.

However, there is a door in front of you that you've never opened before. This door requires courage, and it is the door to your future. Your future is calling your name in gentle whispers. Imagine your name being called right now. However, you were sitting on your sofa of pain. The sofa feels safe only because it's familiar; however, the chair is not comfortable. It's torn up! There's barbed wire sticking out from it, and it is itchy. It is itchier than a mosquito bite, for that matter! Nevertheless, you still sit in it because it's your chair. It's your reminder. It's yours to keep and carry.

What happens with some of us is that even when we step off the sofa to open the door, we bring the old, ragged chair with us. Here's a Public Service Announcement: your future doesn't want the chair; it just wants You! However, you find a way to make it fit through the door. Now Imagine the door being narrow, and it is therefore not meant for the chair to come. There's only enough room for you. However, because you're so connected to the chair, you find a chainsaw to carve out spaces in the door so that you can bring the chair along. You're determined to keep that chair huh?

You move into a new house, and you bring the sofa with you. The sofa takes up space in this new house. It sticks out like a sore thumb. It doesn't elevate your new things, nor does it give them room. You move to Hawaii or Bali, to physically distance yourself and create new memories, yet you still bring the ragged uncomfortable sofa. It takes up space within you wherever you go, which inhibits you from experiencing the future or the present in a fully maximized way because there's a part of you that is still in the chair.

As silly as it sounds, this is what many of us do. We're carrying around the old torn-up barbed wire sofa wherever we go. **The sofa is there when we are alone by ourselves, and it's also there when we try to create new experiences.** Unless you decide to get rid of a sofa that no longer serves you, it will affect the new experiences you create. If we are unable to control our emotions, our emotions will get the best of us. Controlling our emotions and forgiveness is essential for us to experience peace and purpose and live in the present moment. Many of the emotions that come up for us include anger, sadness, grief, fear, and shame. If your emotions control you, you are denying yourself the possibility of bouncing back from setbacks. Understand that there will be setbacks and conflicts. However, it is not meant for that conflict to keep you stagnant. Again, it is possible for you to age but maintain the emotional intelligence of a child, if you have not learned how to control how to experience and control your emotions.

Again, your emotions are not a bad thing. Emotions are central to your humanity. They help you to remain connected with God and others. It was God's love that led to His creation of us. It was also God's love that led to Him dying for us. He loved us while we were yet sinners; Christ died for us. God's ability to care but not be controlled by His emotions provided the ultimate redemption for our sins. Jesus experienced constant grief due to the sinful nature of humankind. Jesus and John the Baptist were very close.

When John the Baptist died, Jesus cried out. He was hurt! Nevertheless, Jesus did not let His emotions get the best of Him or keep Him from His divine purpose. When He was in prayer in the garden of Gethsemane, Jesus knew that His time had come to be crucified. It is said that He cried blood. This is a condition that is represented by high anxiety. He didn't complain about it to His friends. He didn't harbor resentment. He prayed, and He prayed for hours. He knew that the algorithm to keep His heart open was plugging and to God. If Jesus' feelings and emotions led Him, it would have been a deterrent to Him for fulfilling His purpose on earth.

I recall many instances of being led by my emotions. I would constantly argue with my mother and my spouse because I felt that I had to have the last word and wanted to be understood. I would also feel like the victim in these situations due to feeling misunderstood and not releasing issues from the past. Anytime I wanted to resolve a new problem, I would operate from the proximity of a pain point from the past. For example, if I were to address something today, I would use points from when I was offended three years ago or even five years ago.

The sofa I was carrying was evident and would appear in my conversations. I had grown to be irritated and frustrated so quickly and had ironically begun to reflect some of the same behaviors that I was vexed by others when would exhibit those behaviors. Do you know that verse that says remove the plank from your eye before judging others? Yeah, I need it to remove the plank. The best way to transform any relationship is by first changing yourself. Many things that irritate us about other people are the things that we do or the things that we've worked hard to eliminate from our own lives. This is another way of saying that if you are experiencing a complicated relationship with someone, look introspectively and wait to see how you might be participating or helping to create what is reflected. Removing the plank from our own eyes allows us to see more objectively than subjectively. When you're focused on your pain and anger, it is harder for you to know how to positively influence the situation.

I hadn't realized until a certain point in my life that it was possible to confront issues caringly without yelling or being condescending. I thought that conflict and out-of-control emotions were the only way to address issues. Therefore, I would either sweep problems under the rug because I didn't want to experience the pain of confrontation. Or I would implode and express issues from a frustrated place because I couldn't keep them in anymore. Neither action serves me or my relationships.

Have you ever heard of the saying that hurt people hurt people? This is so true. When you are harboring pain and resentment, it is projected onto others. Again we are all on our journey and are at different levels. However, the first place to start is by engaging in self-work. Work on yourself. God says to cast your care upon the Lord because He cares for you. He wants you to release the pain, so you can be present instead of ruminating in the past. Doesn't this sound good? No one openly says, "Today, I want to meditate on past interactions and be depressed or anxious!" However, we do this with our actions, and we normalize it. However, your peace is your responsibility. It is your responsibility to pray and allow God to heal you. God's Word says that He will give you a Divine peace that the world cannot show you.

.

PEOPLE PLEASING INSTEAD OF FINDING PEACE

I can recall trying to find value in what I would do for others, but wouldn't have peace. My motives weren't right. This would keep me from experiencing joy as well because I was constantly exhausted and I had built up resentment. I only saw myself as a caregiver and would blame others because I didn't feel I was receiving the help I wanted.

I'm reminded of Jesus being tempted in the desert during the 40-day fast. Remember, I mentioned how the enemy challenged Him to prove who He was, and instead of doing so, Jesus resisted the temptation. He didn't need to prove to the enemy who He was because He already knew who He was in God.

Nevertheless, many of us are trying to prove ourselves to our family members or people who say what we're not. Constantly trying to "prove to others that I'm good enough," contradicted what God already said in His Word about me. Therefore, I was working against myself and felt tired. I remember the beginning of my marriage was complicated. I love my mother-in-law, and we have a good relationship today, but our relationship wasn't always this way.

My mother-in-law and father-in-law, like most parents, wanted the best for their children. I had a child out of wedlock and came into the relationship with my spouse with my child. I was a single parent, and my spouse was just a single man. His parents felt that we were not a good match for each other because of the dynamics of our relationship. Although I would say now that it was nothing personal. Back then, I would constantly feel that it was judgmental and personalized the pain of what I thought they felt about me. There were instances of disagreements and hurtful words, but essentially everything would fit right with my self-perception. I harbored resentment because I felt that they were unable to see my potential and purpose, even though it wasn't meant for them to see it. I placed them on a pedestal that only God belonged upon. That was on me.

Furthermore, I began to think of different ways to prove how I was "the one" for my spouse. I remember making a list in my mind of all of the beautiful things I would do as a lovely and admirable Proverbs 31 Woman. "I will cook and clean every single day," so I thought. "I would make him smoothies and excellent dinners. I will vacuum and clean every day and keep things spotless. I would wear my little apron and be like Betty Crocker. I would make him happy, and it would be a fairytale." However, in doing so, I became very exhausted and resentful. I realized that I wasn't doing this for him. It was really to prove someone else wrong, but I over-compensated because of my own internal issues. Get what I'm saying?

Y'all, I was trying to prove somebody wrong that didn't even live in my house! My self-perception and the agreements that I made about other people's opinions affected my state of being. Also, doing these things and being motivated by the wrong reason led me to become exhausted and resentful towards my spouse. This was unwarranted. He didn't ask me to do all of these things. I rationalized it in my mind and always said to myself, "Well it needs to be done, and who else is going to do it?" I would do it, which essentially taught him how to treat me by constantly doing. I made myself into this superwoman but did not feel so super on the inside. However, this was because I didn't know my value. I felt tiny on the inside. Due to me holding on to the rugged sofa, I became defensive and divisive even though I truly wanted unity and companionship the most.

The interesting thing is I was not communicating that I wanted help. When I did speak, it was from a frustrated place. Therefore, my emotion would be heard, **instead** of my words. My message would constantly be missed or mistaken. This also added to the frustration and a belief that I created about being misunderstood. I rationalized not to communicate in the first place. **Sofa!** Many times we end up making agreements with negative core beliefs due to our previous experiences. It wasn't until I began praying, fasting, and communicating with care, that my defenses lessened and unity was created between my spouse and I. It's made such a difference!!! **Is there luggage that you need to release? Are there relationships in your life that you'd like to be transformed?**

OUR GOD IS A JUST GOD

Our God is a just God. When you follow God's ways, He will direct your path, protect you and be your vindicator. God says in His Word that you shall not have any other gods before Him. He is the only one and true all-powerful and all-knowing God. When you trust God and your ways please Him, He will even make your enemies be at peace with you (Proverbs 16:7). He will also make your enemies your footstool (Psalms 110:1). I certainly do not regard any people or persons in my family as enemies. However, how can we be unified with each other if our emotions are centered in resentment? Resentment can lead to adversarial relationships. We then begin to treat each other like enemies, even though we desire love in our relationships. God's ways and His Word direct us to release our pain to Him, and He will take it from there.

When you look back at the children of Israel and everything they experienced as the Egyptian's slaves, it was God who knew the right way to handle the circumstances that would allow for change to happen. As we know, God sent horrific plagues to show His mighty hand. He is the one true God, and there are consequences for anyone who challenges this or messes with His children. The Word says that we are not struggling against flesh and blood but principalities. This reminds us that we must go to God in prayer to ask for divine orchestration with the spiritual warfare going on around us. It is an enemy that is constantly waiting to use the emotions and mindset of people to create chaos, confusion, and disruption. It is necessary that we go to God and pray to handle these spiritual attacks.

If we are vindictive and resentful, then our energy to empathize and keep us connected to our purpose will be disrupted. The enemy is the author of lies and disconnection from God and our calling.

Anytime we're feeling disconnected and isolated, the enemy is grinning. However, when you pray for peace over situations and ask God to direct you on how to present your body as a living sacrifice, you are slapping the grin off of the enemy's face! Greater is He that is in you than he that is in the world, and you are more than a conqueror. You are not the negative events or experiences that happened to you. You are the resilience that rises above it. However, to be resilient, you must run to God. **Run To God In Prayer!** God is so just that He will take a situation and turn it around for His glory, and He will use you to do His work.

Let's look back at Joseph and his brothers. His brothers sold Joseph into slavery. This was because his brothers were jealous of Joseph, as we know. However, Joseph was elevated by God. God's favor on his life did not dissipate, even though Joseph endured negative circumstances. As Joseph leaned into God and remained connected to Him, God's plan for him continued to prevail. If Joseph allowed his emotions to get the best of him and allowed his resentment to direct his actions, he wouldn't have been promoted by God while also experiencing God's divine peace. What the enemy planned for evil, God used it for good! His brothers then needed Joseph, who became the director of sustenance during the famine. Without Joseph, they could have starved. Joseph went from the DITCH to DIRECTOR (Genesis 41: 37-44)!

Let's also look at the example of Hagar (Genesis 16: 7-13). God told Abraham that he would be the father of many nations. This was at a time when Sarah was in her 90s. Sarah laughed at this prophecy, and God called her out on it. She quickly dismissed this as the cause of her laughter, but her faith began to diminish as she had not yet conceived.

She then orchestrated her maidservant to sleep with Abraham. Her maidservant then conceived. Eventually, Sarah conceived but grew to be resentful towards Hagar. As Hagar's son grew, Sarah became even more resentful and began to mistreat Hagar and her son. One day, Hagar left and went into the wilderness and began to cry out. God sent an angel to address her. Hagar was certainly not meant to be in the picture based on God's plan and promises, and she didn't ask to be mistreated. She didn't try to put herself in between God's plan for Sarah to give birth. However, she experienced the wrath of her master. Because of Sarah's insecurity and pain, Sarah projected it onto Hagar. This hurt Hagar. Nevertheless, she cried out to God, and God heard her cry and blessed her and her son.

She gave this name to the LORD who spoke to her: "You are the God who sees me," for she said, "I have now seen the One who sees me (Genesis 16: 13)." If God can hear the cry of someone who didn't fit the "plan" and was shunned because of the "dynamics" of the situation, God can hear you and me. Many children come into this world unplanned. I worked with someone who was born out of an affair. Both her mother and biological father were married to other people. She was the public result of what they did in secret. Nevertheless, they treated her as if she had been a secret for many years. They would project anger and pain onto her that led her to develop depression and anxiety. She often would question her existence and identity. Where do I belong? Where do I fit? She certainly didn't ask to be on this earth but was meant to feel that she shouldn't have been born. She'd be told not to talk about how she was born because of fear of bringing shame to the family or fear of judgment. Even though she desired belonging, she hid in fear and conditioned herself to carry the burden of a decision that wasn't her responsibility. She would suppress her own needs and emotions, which created and exacerbated her depression and anxiety. She wasn't a part of their secret plan. Nevertheless, she was a part of God's plan and purpose!

Many children are born into situations that are not conducive to a nurturing and loving home. As mentioned before, the parents who are raising them are often dealing with their own pain and misery that they end up projecting onto the children. The parents have often experienced that same level of mistreatment as well. This creates the pathology of pain being passed down from generation to generation. Again, what we then learn about ourselves, is often a misrepresentation of who we are in Christ. No, we didn't ask to be mistreated, we didn't ask to be born, we didn't ask to be brought up in poverty, we certainly didn't ask for socio-economic challenges or racism.

However, imagine if Hagar didn't plug into God and cry out to Him to deliver her from pain and her circumstances. She could have passed on the pathology of pain to her son. Many times we missed a step. The key to stopping a pathology and generational curses is to see that change can occur by knowing that God is on your side! **God hears the misfits, misunderstood, marginalized, and He does a miraculous work in them!** His glory will be revealed in anyone willing to plug into Him!

CHAPTER 4

DEVELOPING YOUR RELATIONSHIP WITH GOD

GOD IS THE DIRECTOR

"A relationship with God is the MOST important relationship you can have!" — Unknown

Why are we so easily discouraged, and why do we experience doubt? Have you ever asked yourself this question? Interestingly enough, I believe that the answer is tied to your relationship with God. God is the director of your life. However, if you are disconnected from God or divided from Him due to your flesh or actions, this can create discouragement and delay in the opportunities you are supposed to have.

Opportunities come in many different shapes and sizes—new people in your life, jobs, projects, etc. However, disconnection brings or perpetuates disruption. Remember, God warns us that we will experience trials and tribulation. The enemy is in this world to create and perpetuate the chaos. Therefore, trouble is inevitable. This means that we must stay on guard through prayer. God talks about putting on the whole armor of God so that we can go into battle spiritually. He didn't mean to put on full armor to start fights with people and kill them (verbally or physically). He is telling us that we need to stay prayerful.

He gives us the keys to unlock power and perseverance. Whatever is loose on Earth will be released in Heaven (Matthew 16:19). He is waiting on us to pray for His divine orchestration and facilitation, so we can be set free. Remember, God gives us free will because He loves us. It is up to you to understand what His keys and tools are by reading His Word. The keys and tools that He gives us revolve around prayer, fasting, reading, and implementing His Word. Your connection with God is essential to your relationship with your purpose and peace. If you are disconnected from God, you are disconnected from your purpose and peace. We are experiencing a mental health crisis. I believe that this mental health crisis is rooted in the etiology of family issues/trauma, issues encountered outside of the family, and spiritual warfare. Our mindset and response to those issues determine our experience of life. Have you ever heard someone say it's all about perspective? You can either see the glass half empty or half full. Well, this is true. God gives us the tools that will help us cope with any experience to empower us to keep moving forward. **You are meant to move forward.**

WHAT IS PRAYER?

Prayer is talking to God and making your requests known to Him with thanksgiving. His Word says to be anxious for nothing, but make your prayer and supplication be known to God with thanksgiving (Philippians 4:6). God's Word says that there is no need for you to be anxious or fret about anything now or in the future. When your energy is consumed by concerns and worries, it is hard to be present. You're thinking about the future, which is taking away from your experience right now. I can go to any of the most amazing places on Earth, such as Hawaii, Bali, and sit in front of the ocean but not see its beauty.

My mind could be so consumed with negative thoughts stemming from present or past issues. I'm not immersed in joy at that moment because my thoughts are channeled into something negative.

Prayer is making a decisive choice to take action by making your requests be known to God and trusting that He will orchestrate and facilitate everything under His plan. **Wherever our energy goes, it grows.**

With more prayer comes more power! God wants our connection with Him to be so strong that nothing penetrates it. The enemy constantly wants to develop schemes to distract us and disrupt our relationship. Therefore, praying without ceasing is no joke. You need to pray throughout the day. Yes, we have things to do, work, and other responsibilities; however, it is not difficult to acknowledge God throughout the day. It is not difficult to say, "thank you" to God in your mind, or "I need help God."

Many of us are spending time on social media, for instance. We may spend hours binge-watching shows when we come home. Some of us will force our relaxation by drinking alcohol or doing drugs. This is due to the lack of peace and the desire to forcefully calm down the rehearsing of negative thoughts in one's mind. However, these maladaptive ways of dealing with pain, anxiety, or fear are neither healthy nor conducive to your purpose. We are turning these things into idols by prioritizing them over prayer. God does not like that, nor is it apart of our design. Not understanding our design leads to the misuse and abuse of ourselves. This then leads to the misuse and abuse of things like drugs and people!

These things do not even work. They may provide a very short relief. However, it leads to long-term emotional disability. We are creatures of habit and develop habits quite quickly; our neurological pathways crave habits. It is easy to form positive and negative patterns. This is done in the repetition and practice of something over and over again. As we repeat this practice, we become more and more committed to it, even if it's a practice that doesn't truly serve us. As a result, we can practice having a distracted lifestyle due to habitually picking up our phones and checking our social media accounts constantly. Once we hear a notification, it's like we must instantly check our phone to see if we won the lottery. We're filling up the void and emptiness that we have on the inside with external validation. We're posting pictures of fake smiles to develop a social circle that is superficial and on the surface.

Furthermore, we may also want to get away from the perceived pressures of life due to feeling so overwhelmed with adult stuff and adulting. People-pleasing behaviors are also rooted in the lack of trust in God and His Holy Spirit within us. We feel the need to perform for others, which is exhausting. As a result, we may have different tasks accumulate, leading to procrastination due to feeling overwhelmed. Binge-watching a show on Netflix or Prime video suddenly becomes very appealing.

First, we're complaining about not having enough time in the day, but what are we using our time on? This is what happens when we're consumed by worry. Stephen Covey talks about the area of concern and influence in his book *The 7 Habits of Highly Successful People*. He expresses that many of us are spending 80% of the time in our area of concern and only 20% in our area of influence. Our area of concern represents the things that we are worried or anxious about. These are the things that are beyond our control. As a result of spending so much time here, our ruminations about it grow. Imagine shifting towards your area of influence. These are the things that are in your control.

Prayer is in your possession. Imagine praying more than worrying. Again, the scripture says to be anxious for nothing. God already knows our needs. He doesn't want us to murmur and complain. He wants us to develop confidence and trust in Him to supply all of our needs according to His riches in glory (Philippians 4:9). Pray more and worry less. This is key.

WHAT IS FASTING?

Fasting is a divine tool in which we abstain from the fleshly desires we are accustomed to and have grown a routine around. Again, because we are creatures of habit, it is easy for us to become desensitized to something not serving us. We can be easily influenced and persuaded if we are not plugged into God. Plugging into God is key to hearing His direction, instruction, and correction. If we're not plugged into God, we can be easily tempted and persuaded.

As I mentioned before, if you are not plugged into God, then what are you plugged into? Another way of asking this is if God is not influencing you, then what are you being affected by? The effects of social media, certain music and people can lead to perversion, procrastination, and other negative behaviors. All of these things share some level of influence and can affect your spirit. Fasting is the willful abstaining from all of these things so that you can replace the time that you would spend on these things with prayer, worship, and reading God's Word. You then form a new habit and lifestyle by decisively and intentionally connecting with God longer and more often. Fasting breaks the yokes of bondage that we have created due to our habitual nature. Do you need freedom from habitual sin? Do you need freedom from sexual immorality and perverse behavior? Do you need freedom from lying and being led by fear? Do you need freedom from social media? Do you need freedom from drug use? Do you need freedom from your emotions? Fasting and prayer are key to God breaking the yokes and chains to all of these things that I have named and more.

In God's Word, there was a story in which the disciples were praying for a boy who was possessed by evil spirits. Jesus was a few feet away praying. Jesus had already developed a lifestyle of prayer and fasting and knew the importance of the tools to maintain His connection to God and fulfill His calling. The disciples were praying fervently. I mean, they were going in with all they could! I can imagine them huffing, puffing, and laboring in prayer, yet the boy was not being delivered. Jesus came and said "out" and instantly the boy was set free from all of the demonic spirits.

The disciples were quiet. I imagine that they were confused by why their prayers hadn't worked. Later on, Peter developed the courage to ask Jesus about what happened and why their prayers hadn't helped set the boy free. Jesus responded by saying, this kind comes out not just by prayer but by prayer and fasting (Matthew 17:21).

There are some yokes and chains that need to be broken in your life. It has hooked itself on to you and wants to maintain its connection and hold on to you. It wants to cement itself to you so that you stay off course. Fasting is the denial of the things that make you feel good but are not truly good or right for you. It is the willful denial of satisfying the flesh so that you are no longer being led by it. If your flesh can then be tamed and controlled, it weakens the grip and begins to weaken the chain until the chain is broken.

As I shared before, sexual trauma led to me developing negative beliefs about myself. I thought that I was disgusting as what I had experienced was perverted and disgusting. I developed and maintained these beliefs. I had not yet developed a personal relationship with God and was not praying and fasting. I made up my mind that fasting was too hard for me to do. I wanted to have fun and experience instant gratification, even though it didn't take away my pain. My pain was always there, like the torn-up sofa waiting for me to come back. I made a false agreement, that temporary relief was better than no relief at all because I did not understand the power of prayer and fasting and the relief that it could bring me. Nor did I try to understand it.

Many of us pride ourselves on being Christians, but anytime we try to handle things our own way not in accordance with God's Word, we are essentially no different than atheists. The Word of God says He would rather us be hot or cold for Him, but not lukewarm (Revelation 3:15-16). He doesn't want us in between. He wants us to go all-in for Him because that is essential to living our purpose daily. Nevertheless, I recycled negative thoughts of myself and outsourced my need for love and validation through various romantic relationships. None of these relationships would work out in my favor, as I would attract men who were in alignment with the negative thoughts I had of myself. They essentially couldn't love me in the way that I was looking for. I needed to plug into the ultimate source of love to know love truly. However, my bar was so low that anyone who could compliment me or pay attention was like a knight in shining armor.

I didn't ask to be sexually traumatized as a child. I previously discussed how this led to me recreating trauma in my life, but I also created emotional trauma and spiritual attacks against my purpose, until I got the help I needed and prayer, therapy, and fasting. The enemy wanted to use the trauma that I experienced as a way to keep me disconnected from God and my purpose. The enemy wanted me to see myself through the lens of my experience. I refused to use the keys that God had given me, which led to me repeating the same mistakes repeatedly.

It was through reconnecting with God and taking my relationship with God seriously, that allowed me to heal and experience peace and His love. The pattern of seeing myself through sexual objectification perpetuated for years. The pattern of people-pleasing behavior and hiding my true self because of thinking I wasn't good enough also lasted for years. Prayer keeps us connected to God, but again His Word says, "This kind only comes out not just by prayer but by prayer and fasting." The traumatized part of me wanted to stay within me. The sofa did not want to leave the house. The sofa wanted to grow roots as if it were a tree.

However, God destroys yokes. We must be willing to willfully abstain from how we do things so that God's divine intervention can pull out the weeds and roots. It is by God's grace and my journey of intentional healing that I am healed! I am a living representation of what God can do. I experienced negative thoughts, maybe even thousands of negative thoughts each day about myself. Some studies say that we experience up to 6000 thoughts a day. That is a lot of thinking. These are automatic thoughts that occur and are connected to the beliefs that you have about yourself. Are you keeping count of the number of thoughts you have? No. So it may surprise you that you are even thinking that much. Nevertheless, you are! Do you see why prayer without ceasing and living a fasted lifestyle isn't too much to ask for? You need prayer throughout the day and constant fasting to overpower the negative thoughts and principalities that want to infiltrate your spirit. Make this a lifestyle, and you shall remain set free!

MY STEPS ARE ORDERED BY GOD!

It is essential and so important to obey the call of God. Do you remember the story of Jonah and the whale? Jonah was an emotional prophet who heard from God but wanted to do things his way. Jonah had his plan in mind and did not want to go where God told him to speak to the people. As a result of doing things his way, God sent a whole whale to come and swallow him. Jonah stayed in the whale's mouth for a few days as a consequence of his actions. Jonah then decided that he would yield to God. He cried out to God in prayer. Jonah's disobedience to God led him away from his purpose. Surrendering to God got him back on track with God's plan. The story didn't end there.

Jonah didn't understand why God wanted to send him as a spokesperson on His behalf to lead the people to redemption. Jonah preferred the people to die instead of being saved by God. Jonah felt that their actions deserved persecution and God's retribution. Initially, Jonah's motives and emotions led him, which created an internal resistance before he finally participated in God's plan. Jonah's initial perspective inhibited him from seeing the possibilities of God's plan, as he was more committed to his emotional immaturity.

Many of us have been Jonah at one point. Because of our pain and disappointment with our plans not working in the way we want them to, we become jealous or miserable. Jonah did not want the people to be saved and prosper due to his pride and ego. His pride kept him emotionally and spiritually stifled.

Nevertheless, God's plan will always prevail! There are consequences for not yielding to God when He calls us. Yes, God has given us will, but He also intended for us to remain connected to Him and pray for His will to be our will. He did not mean for us to allow the pain and disappointment of our experiences to fester in our souls and spirit. When it does, it keeps us from seeing or being connected to God's design. The path that God has designed for us is uncharted territory. He is usually taking us on different pathways that we've never been before, which can be daunting. We may feel hurt and don't want others to prosper due to where we are in life. Or we may be fearful of going where God is calling us to. This is a result of insecurities that perpetuate doubt, shame, fear, and discouragement.

However, disobedience leads to disarray and chaos in our lives. This opens us up to living self-sabotaging lifestyles. When we don't learn the lessons and yield to God, we recreate experiences that affect us and our relationships. As we are being held back by ourselves, we simultaneously hold up other people around as well. Our lack of control of ourselves leads us to want to control the outcome of other people.

I was listening to this poem one day in which the writer had identified the negative part of himself as a monster wolf. He created this poem to honor the women of the Me Too Movement, who had shared a commonality of experiencing hiding their light and living in a shadow of negative beliefs about themselves due to what happened to them. He talks about how the offender is the wolf who projects his anger onto the victim due to his insecurities and himself. The light of the woman he hurt shined a light on his insecurities, making him uncomfortable. He didn't like it, so he did everything in his might to blow out her light.

Plugging back into God and yielding to God is key to healing so that we are not hurting ourselves and others. I remember multiple points in my adult life in which I felt so convicted by how my emotions would lead me. In spite of the conviction, I would repeatedly let my feelings manage me instead of me controlling them. As a result, I would create distance and pain between myself and the people closest to me. However, I found a scripture that stuck out to me that stated, "Better is a dry morsel and quietness therewith, than a house full of sacrifices with strife (Proverbs 17:1)." I can spend money and buy things for the people that I love. I can clean the house like it's nobody's business. I can put my foot in my cooking and make it taste so good, but if I continue to disobey God's Word and handle matters with contentious, all of those things I am doing are in vain. It is better to have nothing and be peaceful than to have everything with resentment. Let me say that again for all of the wives and mothers out there. It's better to have nothing and be peaceful than have everything and do everything for everyone with resentment.

Your house is meant to be a house of peace, not a place of chaos. The more you are committed to being obedient to God's Word and His calling for you, the more you are committed to your peace and purpose. Obedience to God's Word and prayer raises a standard and elevates you. Elevation requires separation from anything that is not of God and any negative emotion that may be within you. With elevation, God will comfort you on all sides. Psalm 71:21

Disobedience drives brokenness. However, remember that God is the ultimate restorer and redeemer. Many of us are not used to the elevation that healing comes with. Healing in the process of being in your purpose can even be uncomfortable. You may have been hidden for so long that being in your light and being more visible is utterly daunting. Your old framework may hit you with resistance when your true self is coming out because it wants to remind you of when you were hurt the last time you put yourself out there. It wants to remind you of the painful experiences that visibility brought before, such as abandonment, rejection, sexual, physical, and emotional trauma. However, obeying God's Word allows His light to shine through you, that when people see you, they see God. Then they will want to come to Him and know Him for themselves. That through you, God's glory will be revealed! You were always a part of the plan and you are the salt and light of the world!

OBEDIENCE PROTECTS US

Obedience is another form of God protecting us from the wrong people and things. When we obey His Word and His ways, it protects us from being misguided by bad influences. I remember being a pre-teen and teenager and being more concerned with popular opinion than God's plan to preserve me. I was focused on "protecting my-self from rejection" by being accepted by the masses. There is one instance in which I thought I was being godly, but I would hang out with the wrong crowd to fit in. We were all hanging out in my friend's cousin's apartment. His mother owned the apartment and she was not the best influence. They were all smoking marijuana, including her. I was probably 13 or 14, and my friend was around the same age. Her cousin was male and was perhaps 15 or 16. I believe his mother provided the marijuana. I watched everyone as they smoked. They of-fered it to me, and I declined. They all knew that it wasn't something I was into, and there was no pressure involved. The male cousin of my friend made a joke saying, "Yes, we're smoking, but Mimi is going to die first". Hahaha, they all laughed. I didn't think this was funny, but I forced my laughter as well. It was all about fitting in for me! What sad irony is this?

I wasn't smoking, but I was inhaling second-hand smoke, which I hear is often worse. Being a part of a crowd that wasn't for me was not only killing me physically, but it was killing my purpose. The Word of God says he who tries to save his life loses, and he who gives his life to Christ finds it (Luke 17:33). When you first read that Scripture, it can be very challenging to understand it when you're looking at it from your fleshly eyes. One would think, why wouldn't I want to save my own life? This Scripture means that you lose it when you try to preserve your own life by your own means instead of fol-lowing God. You lose sight of who you are in Christ because you're becoming those who are around you and you "LOSE YOURSELF".

Disobedience leads to self-sabotage. However, when you give your life to Christ, you find life aligned with your creator! God wants to provide you with life and give you life more abundantly!

CHAPTER 5

FRUITS OF THE SPIRIT

GOD'S NATURE

"Every Problem is a Character Building Opportunity!"—Rick Warren

To understand your true self, you must be committed to understanding God's nature. After all, God designed mankind in His image. Mankind doesn't refer to your sexual identity as a male or female. It refers to all of us, our species. Mankind refers to God's Holy Spirit within us. I mentioned before, that our world is facing an identity crisis. Some of us constantly want to be like the next person because, on the surface, it appears that what we see in them is something that we don't have. However, are they producing good fruit? The Scripture says in Matthew 7:15-20 (NKJV):

15 "Beware of false prophets, who come to you in sheep's clothing, but inwardly they are ravenous wolves.

16 You will know them by their fruits. Do men gather grapes from thornbushes or figs from thistles?

17 Even so, every good tree bears good fruit, but a bad tree bears bad fruit.

18 A good tree cannot bear bad fruit, nor can a bad tree bear good fruit.

19 Every tree that does not bear good fruit is cut down and thrown into the fire.

20 Therefore by their fruits you will know them.

Sometimes we see individuals with many likes on social media, or they appear to be glorifying fancy cars/clothes, etc. However, on the inside, they are hurting and are actually exhausted with maintaining a certain appearance solely for the "likes."

Focusing on the inward parts, and building a character based on the fruits of the spirits, will reveal who God has uniquely called you to be!

LOVE

What is love? Love is God. Love does not control us. Love prospers us. Love is sacrificial, compassionate, and holds us accountable when we steer in the wrong direction. Love corrects us. Love is unconditional. Love redeems us. God is the definition of love. There is no love without God.

God is constantly thinking of us and is sacrificial. I remember growing up and hearing the saying that love hurts. Love does not hurt. Humanity hurts. If mankind is not plugged into God, the enemy's influences can perpetuate harm, evil, and disconnection with God. However, God's love never fails us. Jesus was battered and bruised for our iniquities and took on the curse of sin for our redemption. He sacrificed Himself for us so that we can experience freedom from sin. God says in His Word that we do not have to be controlled by sin or principalities. Yielding to God and understanding Him grants us the freedom to understand our true selves in God. God's Word says that they that worship me must worship me in spirit and truth (John 4:24). This means that the old self must be released. The old self is the false sense of self. Behold old things have passed away and behold new things have come (2 Corinthians 5:17). We are new creatures when we profess that God is real and accept God in our lives.

We're often looking for people and things to fill the void we experience daily. We then become frustrated when these sources do not work out. We place these big expectations on individuals that do not understand how to love. They may also be experiencing pain from their past that limits their capacity to give love because they have not given or released their pain to the ultimate Comforter. As we're making conscious decisions to receive love from God and obey His Word in a way that keeps our hearts open, God is filling every void which permits us to share His passion and give love. One of the biggest challenges we all face is the desire for companionship while also not wanting to experience the possibility of being hurt again. This is because we are unsure if we will be okay if we are disappointed by someone else's actions.

Those painful parts of me took up some of my heart's capacity to experience God's love and show it. However, God's love conquers all. God's love will cast out fear (1 John 4:18). Fear brings torment. God's love brings peace.

2 Timothy 1: 7 says, "I have not given you a spirit of fear, but power, love, and a sound mind." Why does He point out power, love, and a sound mind? Because these are the things that we experience challenges with the most. If we don't quickly release those negative emotions, we then allow them to rule over us. Allowing God to take over permits the experience of His spirit, power, healing love, and a stable mind. Furthermore, God is not a man that He should lie (Numbers 23:19). He wants you to experience power, love, and a sound mind, as these are the essence of stability despite all odds. If you and I have an "I will be okay no matter what mindset," you will be open to all of the

possibilities of what God has in store for you rather than being stuck in negative thought patterns. **Plug into Him=Plug into Love.**

PEACE

What is peace? The best way to describe peace is by first describing the chaos that life brings. Life can many times be a hurricane with strong winds tossing you to and fro. Again, God's Word asserts that you will experience tribulation (John 16:33). The enemy is here to steal, kill, and destroy. Just like Hurricane Katrina came here to destroy everything in its path. The enemy main intent is to uproot and bring disconnection and division. However when you are grounded in God and you make a decisive choice to not allow anything to separate you from His love, then you will not be moved. I heard this one analogy that spells this out so well. There's a reason why buildings crumble and fall when strong winds come, but trees do not. This is because the roots of the trees are so deeply plugged into the ground, in a way that keeps it standing. God will give you peace in the eye of the storm by remaining rooted in Him. A hurricane, in spite of its winds reaching hundreds of miles an hour on the outside destroying everything in its path, has a center that is very calm. This amazes me every time I think about it. How can the eye of the hurricane be peaceful?

In the Bible, God often refers to Himself as two animals. An eagle and a lion. In the context of a hurricane, the eagle is the only bird that will fly towards the storm instead of away from it. Why is this? "Fearlessly, the eagle would fly into the fierce winds, using the storm current to rise higher quickly. The pressure of the storm is used to help them glide without using their energy as their wings' unique design allows them to lock in a fixed position amid the violent storm winds. The eagle instinctively knows it: Just past the storm, in the high heavens, there is peace and security. It is the perfect hiding place."— P Holbrook.

Pulling this into a spiritual revelation when we activate God's Presence in our lives by praying, we are also activating peace. It is being in our area of concern and anxiety that drives us into overworking ourselves. Anytime we are experiencing chaos and tribulation, see it as an opportunity to rest in God's arms.

God will give you a peace that the world cannot give you and a peace of the world cannot take away (John 14:27). When things do not go the way we want them to or we experience attacks, we want to blame God. But why blame God for the perverse ways of mankind or for our own shortcomings? Remember, God's plan is not to harm us. Our generation can act so entitled to want what we want and when we want it. In this case, we wouldn't be able to handle the things of God because we're not operating according to the **pulse** of God. Instead, we are led by **impulsivity.**

"But those who hope in the LORD will renew their strength. They will soar on wings like eagles; they will run and not grow weary, they will walk and not be faint" Isaiah 40:21. If you're not experiencing peace in any situation, always go back to God as a rule of thumb. Ask God for revelation and insight. Also remember, God is waiting on you. **He wants to give you peace.**

WORKING AGAINST PEACE

Prioritizing the opinions of other people constantly led me to be in opposition of my own peace. I would prioritize their opinions over God's viewpoint of me. I was antagonistic towards my peace due to how I had conditioned myself to seek their validation. I was in the passenger seat of the vehicle God gave me, and would let others drive the metaphorical car. These are also the same individuals that I resented because they wouldn't just accept me as I am and not judge me, in spite of me giving them "the car." "But I gave them the car, so why am I not experiencing peace?," I thought. Like the Barbie I mentioned earlier, I allowed them to rule and guide me, even though they didn't know what was best for me. Once you give someone something, that they are not supposed to have authority over, misuse is inevitable! While they were driving, and as I allowed them to "drive my actions and feelings", every pothole and tree was run over and hit! The vehicle was being damaged and abused! I experienced more pain and disappointment than I actually needed to. People do not belong on a pedestal, that ONLY God belongs on! 1 Corinthians 6:19-20 says, "Do you not know that your bodies are temples of the Holy Spirit, who is in you, whom you have received from God? You are not your own; you were bought at a price. Therefore honor God with your bodies." The validation that we actually need, comes from being in God's will and glorifying God with our bodies and whole heart!

I wonder how Mary must have felt when she was told by the angel she would give birth to the son of God, as a virgin. During this time, it would have been heinous for a woman to give birth out of wedlock. In addition to that, the man who was courting her would also likely question how she became pregnant. In this case, we know that the angel visited both Mary and Joseph to prepare them for what was to come. I imagine that both Mary and Joseph feared judgment and rejection. Nevertheless, they allowed God's divine peace to overshadow any fear that they had, so they would be in alignment with their purpose versus misaligned by other people's opinions.

I had a child out of wedlock. I remember being called a statistic and having baggage that another man would not want. I was told that a single man should not engage with a woman who had children. However, people are more apt to judge what they see on the outside versus understanding your trauma and pain. Their judgment of me as an adult was also their judgment of the six-year-old sexually traumatized little girl that was inside of me. My own judgment of my adult behaviors was also my judgment against my six-year-old sexually traumatized little girl inside of me. Sadly, I'd often think about how I could answer God's calling on my life, now that people don't see my potential, as they are focused on my past. I allowed the opinions of other's to drive me off course, however, it was God's divine peace and truth of who I was in God that allowed me to experience a peace that people could not provide me. They simply did not have the capacity to do so. I can't fault them. Faulting and blaming them gives away my power. "I have not given you a spirit of fear, but power, love, and a sound mind."

Adam blamed Eve because it was easier to blame her, than take responsibility for his own actions. God: "Why did you eat the fruit, Adam? Adam said, "Because the woman you put here, gave it to me." What? That's like saying, "Yes you gave me purpose and power, but I'm going to deny that I even have it." Or, "Yes you gave me a vehicle, but I'm going to deny that I let someone else drive it, when you told me to drive it." The children of Israel blamed Moses, which kept them from looking at themselves. If they heard their own murmurings and complaints they too would have been vexed. Moses was vexed by listening to their complaints! They were worse than a broken record! Nevertheless, their blame and complaints kept them in the desert 40 years longer than they were supposed to be. They perpetuated their pain too because they hadn't allowed the peace of God to heal their trauma. They eventually learned this the hard way. Leaning into the peace of God is activating healing in your life! **It's time to get back in the driver seat, and let that holy GPS (the Holy Spirit) guide you.** Remember your "vehicle" belongs to the manufacturer, aka God! In all things, acknowledge Him, and he'lll make your paths straight! I'm not saying there won't be bumps along the way, but there's something about being under the manufacturer's warranty! However, this warranty doesn't have an expiration date, and you'll have more peace of mind, by being under His guidance and protection!

LONGSUFFERING

What is longsuffering? It is having or showing resilience in troubles, especially those caused by other people. Jesus is the epitome of displaying longsuffering. Jesus endured the constant rebuttals, rejections, and resistance of humankind, who hated Him for His righteousness. Living righteously and remaining calm despite the pain that people cause you will also make people unhappy. The enemy wants to get a rise of negative emotions out of you. This is also a part of the enemy's scheme. We often want the ideal outcomes with the least amount of work and preparation in our fast-paced generation. As a result, we lack the capacity and capability to handle the challenges that come with relationships, businesses, etc.

We hurriedly rushed into those things, convincing ourselves of our readiness, even though we never allowed ourselves to learn the lessons or heal from previous experiences. Then once again, self-sabotaging behavior propels us into a crashing car of poor outcomes. In this context, our 6 or 7-year-old self is driving the car while we're in the passenger seat. We hope to get to the destination but cannot see over the steering wheel. We've jumped into a car that is not meant for us and it is bound to crash. "That's not me," you may think. However, this is many of us at one point or another.

Have you ever responded rashly and then thought, "I shouldn't have said that." Have you ever ended a relationship due to a lack of patience? Have you ever mistreated someone simply because they were moving slower than you, not because they wanted to harm you? These are the types of individuals that Jesus dealt with. He dealt with even worse individuals who had no morals or good character. Because Jesus was plugged into God's peace, He was able to withstand the constant attacks and murmurings of different people. Jesus learned how to navigate each conflict by speaking the necessary words that didn't escalate the situation. He knew how to shut down harmful rhetoric and people's disbelief without losing Himself in emotions.

This is a divine skill. It's important to understand that long-suffering doesn't equate to perpetuating the tolerance of negative people in your life or even allowing them to have access to you. Jesus set them straight. Jesus had healthy boundaries that he implemented with his calm yet powerful words and parables. He didn't switch up his rhetoric to please them. He remained focused on what his purpose was. Jesus' resilience helped Him to stay committed to righteousness. Those who hunger and thirst after righteousness, they shall be filled (Matthews 5:6). The key is to remain hungry and thirsty for God so that you can be empowered and resilient despite the trials and tricks of the enemy.

MEEKNESS

Moses is regarded as the meekest man on earth. Moses was also a long sufferer. The children of Israel constantly criticized him. The children of Israel would always complain in the wilderness. Once, they began to mock him by saying that he was the prince of the wilderness. This hurt Moses to his core. Moses, under the instruction of God, led them out of Egypt. He constantly reminded them that God provides and they should not fear.

They also saw many examples of God providing in the wilderness. Manna came out of Heaven. Water came out of rocks. Food was abundant. The children of Israel were conditioned to have a poverty mindset making it hard for them to see and accept the possibilities of God's provision.

Nevertheless, Moses would take every problem to God. Moses was a servant leader. He would hear the cries of the children and in spite of feeling vexed by them, he would mediate between the children of Israel and God. Because of the children of Israel's complaints and immoral behavior, there were times that God became quite upset with them. Once they worshiped an idol, and another time they engaged in sexual immorality. God dealt with them and consumed many with fire and other types of plagues. When you think of it, there was a dichotomy of the children of Israel wanting deliverance but still were obstinate and stubborn in their perspective. They were prisoners to their viewpoint.

Conversely, there's Moses, who is molding himself by God's will and direction. When you look at the picture as a whole, it appears as if everyone is following God, as their leader is guiding them through the wilderness. However, many of them died due to being led by their flesh instead of the direction of God's Spirit.

Of course, this is also mind-boggling to me as God presented Himself as a cloud, guiding them through the wilderness. God was there, and it's as if they knew it not! They saw God in so many different ways and still experienced doubt and disbelief. The Red Sea would have done it for me. The plagues would have done it as well. I would have been like, okay, God; I know you're real. I got you. It's almost like they were so stuck in seeing things subjectively that they were more connected to suffering and sin than they were salvation. Fast forward to today; you can certainly go to church once a week or twice a week, listen to worship music and maybe even pray a few minutes before you eat.

However, if we're not yielding to God and allowing ourselves to mold to the plan that He has for us, we're no different than the children of Israel who were consumed by sin instead of God's salvation.

What He wanted to provide was so clear. I will lead you to a land flowing with milk and honey, said God! What He had was so much better than what they experienced in Egypt as slaves. Moses understood the importance of prioritizing God's plan over his plan. I'm amazed at how direct his communication was with God. It's like they were friends. Moses took everything to God. He knew he needed God to fulfill God's ultimate plan. Being meek allows us to be molded into God's way and plan for our lives.

Once, my husband and I were arguing with one another. I recall being vexed by this. It bothered me so much. I also felt like Moses in some way, and I was tired of the murmurings and complaints. I remembered praying and hearing God's voice so clearly. When I tell you it was so clear, I can't exaggerate. It wasn't my thought; it was His voice. Do you know what God said to me while I was crying and upset? God told me to go and wash my husband's feet. I said, "What? You want me to go and wash his feet?" So I got myself together and prepared this foot spa with warm water.

I took it before my spouse. He was watching television and I asked him if I could wash his feet. This made my spouse uncomfortable because it wasn't anything I'd ever done before. The last time I experienced foot-washing was as a preteen, likely around 12 years old, and we only did this in church.

Nevertheless, God wanted to show me something about my emotions, and He wanted to humble me. If I am so guided by my feelings, it makes it hard and almost difficult to hear God's direction. Any thought and action that we are doing, we're essentially shaping ourselves into it. I was being shaped by contentiousness, which drove me into a place of discouragement and dismay. However, when we give our issues to God, He elevates us and provides us with peace beyond our understanding (Philippians 4:7). This is what He wanted for Moses.

This is what God wants for you and me. It is not meant for you to be controlled by other people's opinions or their murmurings and complaints. You can be a leader, and right under you, there are individuals who are talking about you behind your back and straight to your face. Some of us do not even want to have leadership roles because we feel it's lonely at the top. We are more focused on being with the crowd than we are being set apart. What if God wants to elevate you into a leadership role, but you are resistant to it because you don't want to be talked about? Or what if God wants to take you into a new relationship, but your attitude prevents you from learning how to navigate the difficulties of another person's personality? Dealing with any person will come with problems because people are people. And everyone is on their journey.

Nevertheless, God is the problem fixer, as He is the Master Potter! When we allow God to mold us, it pleases God! His Word says that when a man's ways please God, He makes even his enemies be at peace with him (Proverbs 16:7). Have you ever heard of the saying kill them with kindness? That is what this is about. Humility is not weakness. It is an action that God honors, and He'll convict the person that you're dealing with. That creates more transformative change than us yelling! I will never forget that day when God dealt with my emotions. He opened up my eyes to how I was contributing to the problem and creating escalation. I thank God for being the Master Potter and me being the clay!

WHY AUTHENTICITY REQUIRES NEW BEHAVIORS

Now that you understand some of the fruits of the Spirit, being a new creature in God requires you to activate new behaviors. As I mentioned before, we are creatures of habit. Even when we become saved, after accepting Christ into our lives, we must become intentional about our actions. We must make a lifestyle change. However, to make a lifestyle change, we have to change our mindset and actions. Being Christ-like doesn't just happen on its own without intention.

Jacob was a man who struggled with God. He was more accustomed to how he saw himself and how others saw him. Remember, Jacob was a con artist. He stole his brother's birthright and fled for his life. He spent many years living in fear. Nevertheless, when it was time to leave his father-in-law's house, he was ready to go but was struck with fear. This was because the past was something he did not want to confront. However, for him to move forward, Jacob would have to make peace with the past.

Many of us do not even want to deal with or process what has happened in our history. We're so ready to move forward that we miss vital lessons and don't receive the healing needed to prepare for our future. The past is a part of you, which doesn't mean that the past is you. Therefore many times, we're struggling from day to day because we've not made peace with our history.

God wanted Jacob to have peace. Jacob sent his wives and animals before him, so they could "run into him first." Jacob was afraid of Esau. The last time he saw Jacob, Esau wanted to kill him. The last time Moses saw Egypt, there was a hit on his life. The last time Joseph saw his brothers, they wanted to kill him but sold him into slavery. The past often makes us uncomfortable because we don't know if we can handle what comes with it or not. Nevertheless, if we choose not to confront our past and make peace with it, we're also choosing not to be in our purpose. Purpose requires authenticity and truth, not shame from the past! Shame creates a false sense of self that wants to stay hidden.

Jacob wrestled with an angel. He wrestled with him so much to the point that he took a blow to his hip. Jacob was walking with a limp. Many of us can be like Jacob. We wrestle with God. It takes a blow to open our eyes and understand that our sight has flaws. God told Jacob that his new name was Israel. He gave him an entirely new name to show that the way God sees him is completely different from how he sees himself. The name that you have now is quite different from the name that God has for you. Imagine that. This requires you to be more committed to who you are in Christ than who you knew yourself to be in the past. Once Jacob followed God's direction, he made peace with his brother. God had already touched his brother's heart. God went before Jacob and divinely facilitated their reconnection. Activating new behaviors means trusting God and being confident that He will work things out in your favor. All things work for the good of them that love God and are called according to their purpose (Romans 8:28).

Being authentic requires acceptance of the past. As radical as that sounds, you can't go back and change the past. The past is there, and it's a part of you. Many times we struggle with not wanting to remember the trauma or negative experiences we've had. As a result, we deny ourselves the ability to know that we will be okay. I have worked with some clients who want to change their behaviors now but were reluctant to process the past. Confronting the past is uncomfortable!

Those that confront the past do it uncomfortably, but make progress! Forgetting does not equate to resilience. Sweeping it under the rug does not equate to strength. Courage of confronting the past, is the processing of pain and releasing it, which creates stability. If I'm afraid of a past that has already happened, how can I be open to a future that has not yet happened? I already know what happened in the past. It's up to me to allow myself to process it to release the pain and shift towards possibility. God says in His Word that we can do all things through Christ, which strengthens us (Philippians 4:13).

God is a God of love and opportunity, not avoidance and fear. Being in Christ and being authentic requires you not to be avoidant. He needs you to have compassion and confront the parts of you that have yet to yield to God. He wants to fill those parts with His unconditional love! It requires you to have the courage to evict fear so your purpose can take its place. What matters is the new creature that you are in Christ and how God sees you! Being a new creature in Christ is taking on the identity of Christ and putting old things away, which also means putting the old behaviors away and no longer engaging in them. We're responsible for our commitment to who we are in Christ! Are there any parts of your past that you're afraid to confront? How would your life be different if you did? How would you help you be more authentic?

CHAPTER 6

MAXIMIZE YOUR FREEDOM AND BE BLESSED

"True freedom is only found when one escapes from oneself and enters into the liberty of the children of God."— Francois Fenelon

GOD'S COVENANT

Remember, God has plans to prosper you, not plans to harm you. God's covenant is God's commitment to the plan He has for you if you yield to Him. Nevertheless, it is up to you to be obedient to God so that He can walk you through fulfilling His covenant. Many times, the children of Israel's actions were so immoral that God sought to change the plan. However, as they yielded to God's instructions and warnings, God would restore the covenant that He had for them. Your destiny is your decision. To fulfill the covenant that God has for you requires that you take responsibility for your actions.

God's covenant that He has with you means that you're deciding to perform for an audience of one. King Saul struggled with this, as he started to focus on pleasing the people instead of God. King Saul then got off course and as a result, God's spirit left him and a tormenting spirit came upon him (1 Samuel 16:14). He did not have peace and was filled with jealousy and rage. That audience of one is God and God alone. This eliminates the need or desire to please the tens, hundreds, and thousands of people you may interact with, whether in person or on social media. Ultimately, they are not your audience. They do not have a covenant with you. God does. If you want to operate for your purpose, you must understand this principle. Performing for the audience of one, allows you to work with a spirit of excellence, order, and decency!

The Bible says that everything you do, do it with the spirit of excellence (1 Corinthians 14:40). When you do it with a spirit of excellence, perfection and peace are on the other side. I'm not referring to perfectionism in a way that creates anxiety. I'm referring to being so radical for God that God gives you joy, compassion, and peace in the process. The type of perfection that God refers to will not lead to pain and anxiety.

Many people struggle with perfectionism because they are trying to protect their ego or image. Everything appears perfect on the outside, however, there is constant turmoil on the inside. In the context of people-pleasing behavior and perfectionism, you may see yourself as either a failure or a success. You may overextend yourself because you were trying to prove yourself to other people. This is not even sustainable as people change. There are so many people on this Earth who are dealing with their issues. When performing for them, you're agreeing that you can appease everyone, which is not valid. God Himself, is not about pleasing everyone. God rains on the just as well as the unjust (Matthew 5:45). As I mentioned before, He's no respecter of persons. He looks at everyone's heart, and if they are not in alignment with God, the covenant won't be fulfilled. Again, when we look at Jesus, He was perfect, and yet they crucified Him! We are certainly nowhere near as perfect as Him. We all have sinned and come short of the glory of God.

Nevertheless, He who did no sin was still bruised and battered and spoke down to and hated. He didn't deserve any of that. Nonetheless, Jesus still maintained meekness and allowed Himself to be sacrificed so that the covenant of God would be fulfilled. God wanted us to be free from sin, so he paid the ultimate sacrifice so that we could experience the salvation of God!   The people's criticism didn't matter. Their criticism had nothing to do with Jesus's purpose.

Stepping into my purpose and **answering God's call** was daunting. It's still scary at times. It meant that I had to release the emotional baggage that I had been carrying. A part of that baggage was releasing the prioritization of people's opinions, so I could perform for the audience of one! If you want God's covenant to be fulfilled, perform for the audience of one!

SIN AND IMMORALITY

With God, you can experience freedom from habitual sin and immorality. The Bible says, "Do not be conformed to this world but be transformed by renewing your mind so that you may prove what is pleasing and the acceptable, perfect will of God." Throughout the Bible, God is referring to His will and His plan. Our flesh can easily lead us due to heresy, generational curses, and rejecting God as our Lord and Savior. Paul even said, the Spirit is willing, but the flesh is weak. We are in an age epidemic of increased immorality happening across this world. There is a lot of violence and sexual sin. The people are prioritizing their fleshly pleasures over God's purpose for their lives. As a result, the land is in turmoil. God said to submit to Him, and He will heal the land (Chronicles 7:14). This takes accepting God as your Lord and Savior, prayer, and fasting. It doesn't matter how long you have had a habit, as I said before. All that matters is that you accept Christ and commit to who you are in Christ and not who you were before you met him.

GOD'S LAW

Freedom comes with following God's law. If you don't steal, it keeps you out of jail, right? Not stealing, murdering, and following the direction of the land keeps you from being imprisoned and being able to maintain your freedom. God has rules that He wants us to follow, so we're not oppressed by the yoke of the enemy. Look at the following Ten Commandments:

And God spoke all these words:

2 "I am the Lord your God, who brought you out of Egypt, out of the land of slavery.

Remember who brought you out of the chains of bondage. God did this and He wants to use YOU, like he used Moses and so many others to help set the captives free!

Isaiah 61:1 says, "The Spirit of the Lord GOD is upon me; because the LORD hath anointed me to preach good tidings unto the meek; he hath sent me to bind up the brokenhearted, to proclaim liberty to the captives, and the opening of the prison to them that are bound." It is not meant for the people of God to stay bound up in sin or poverty. It is intended for them to be free and live and experience His covenant of peace!

THE TEN COMMANDMENTS:

1. You shall have no other gods before me or worship images and statues.

God says that you will not have any other God before Him. God is the one true God. Again, this includes not making people your God. If you prioritize their opinions over God's plan, you're creating an idol, and this is breaking His law.

Additionally, worshipping idols is creating divination with God. This creates defilement and affects the behaviors of the people around you. This can lead to generational curses as well because of social learning. When we misrepresent God, we are also teaching others the wrong thing. God does not like that because we are then leading people astray instead of leading people to Him.

2. "You shall not misuse the name of the Lord your God, for the Lord will not hold anyone guiltless who misuses His name."

This is clear. We should not misuse the name of the Lord or mock His name!

3. "Remember the Sabbath day by keeping it holy."

God says to remember the Sabbath and keep it holy. Jesus created the Heavens and Earth for six days, and on the seventh day, He rested. I can understand this one is tricky. What about the officers, nurses, doctors, and those working to make a living to feed their families? Well, in Luke 14:4-7, when Jesus was interacting with the Pharisees and was about to heal a man, the Pharisees questioned and berated Him, stating that He was not following the law. Jesus then asked the Pharisees and experts in the law, "Is it lawful to heal on the Sabbath or not?" But they remained silent. So taking hold of the man, He healed him and sent him on his way. Then He asked them, "If one of you has a child or an ox that falls into a well on the Sabbath day, will you not immediately pull it out?" And they had nothing to say.

4. "Honor your father and your mother so that you may live long in the land the Lord your God is giving you."

What if my father and mother did not honor me? Many of us experience pain, abandonment, criticism, and rejection from our parents or people closest to us. Nevertheless, God is giving us the algorithm to keep our hearts open and protected. With healthy boundaries, it is possible to still maintain the dignity of someone that may have caused you hurt. Forgiving them is key. Forgiveness does not equate to condoning bad behavior. Forgiveness sets you free from any pain you may have endured, and it allows you to prosper and move forward in your purpose instead of being held captive by the pain of injustice.

5. "You shall not kill."

Again, this is very clear. Do not kill. In an aging epidemic of violence, there is so much killing on this land. The killing of the innocent is considered murder. Many of us who lose loved ones due to someone else's actions look to be upset with God and blame Him. However, God's Word is clear. He says do not murder. Humankind perverts their own free will, and destruction happens as a result of it.

6. "You shall not commit adultery."

When you're married, the only person that you are supposed to be sleeping with is your spouse. Also, if your spouse is saying to bring someone else into the marriage, that is not of God. God created Adam and Eve. God didn't create Adam and two Eves. God gave Adam one wife. God gave Eve one husband. It is humankind that has taken matters into their own hands to be exponential in various ways. However, God's example is obvious. God's standard also protects us. Our ways create problems that are not even meant for us.

7. "You shall not steal."

Just because you want something doesn't mean it makes it okay for you to take it from somebody else. You are not supposed to steal. This is very clear. I remember experiencing robbery, and it truly felt like a violation and intrusion of my privacy and safety. This did not feel good whatsoever. Nevertheless, God is the great Vindicator, and I know He has dealt with those individuals. Work for what you need and earn it.

8. "You shall not give false testimony against your neighbor."

Do not lie. God's Word is very clear about this. Please do not make up something false about your neighbor because you do not like them. Be honest and truthful. Honesty and truthfulness keep you in integrity with yourself and in integrity with God. God cares about transparency and Truth. Covering up and masking leads you to be double-minded.

9. "You shall not covet your neighbor's wife."

To sin in the heart, Jesus says, is to lust after a woman or a man in your heart with the desire and will to have immoral sex with them. Ask God to remove all pervertedness and to replace it with purity!

10. "You shall not covet your neighbor's house, or his male or female servant, his ox or donkey, or anything that belongs to your neighbor."

Don't be jealous! Rejoice in others' successes. Your blessings are on the way as you yield to God! Also know that God can redeem and restore you if you renounce and repent of your sins. All have sinned and fallen short of the glory of God (Romans 3:23), which means that no one is perfect. If you have accepted God as your Lord and Savior and struggle with habitual sin, I'd recommend praying about this, and asking God to lead you to mentor, that can help pray for you and provide support and accountability. It's not meant for you to be trapped in sin. Who the Son sets free, is free indeed (John 8:36)!

INHERITANCE AND SPIRITUAL BLESSINGS

Again, God has plans to prosper you and not to harm you. There is an inheritance and spiritual blessings that are just waiting for you as you change your ways and allow yourself to be cultivated in God. Being developed in God allows you to be prepared enough to handle the spiritual blessings that He has for you. Many of us want to receive the benefits without yielding completely. God is waiting on you more than you are waiting on God. Ask yourself, "What am I doing that does not allow me to receive an inheritance that God has set aside?" Is it a mindset shift that you need to have? Is it an action shift that you need to do? Confess the parts of you that have yet to yield to God, and ask God to come in!

Living a righteous lifestyle doesn't mean that you will be exempt from experiencing spiritual attacks or warfare. Nor does it mean that you are going to have the popular vote. You will experience warfare and you will be hated at times. However, prioritizing God's peace over people is the key to being brought closer to your spiritual blessings. Every day is an opportunity to receive a spiritual blessing.

Many times we are thinking of spiritual blessings in terms of something materialistic. However, even peace is a blessing! The righteous will not be forsaken. God will take care of those who seek Him out diligently and want to do His will and work.

I recall experiencing a miscarriage and felt discouraged entirely and in dismay. However, I intentionally gave my pain to God and was able to experience peace. This was after the planning and preparation around welcoming my baby into this world. This was after two months of pregnancy and excitement. This hit me like a ton of bricks!

Nevertheless, I know it was spiritual warfare and that the enemy wanted me to get off track and lose my focus with God. However, giving my concerns to God allowed God to do a work within me that allowed me to experience inner peace in a way that I haven't before. As a leader in my line of work, I needed to be in an emotional state that allows me to serve others. By giving my concerns to God and not sweeping it under the rug, I was able to experience the power of His presence in my work as well. I felt His Spirit touching me and comforting me during my sessions with clients. Being in his presence is so amazing! His grace is sufficient for me, and it is for you as well.

His peace was a spiritual blessing for me. Having His peace is better than having a new house or car even. It seems that this concept is misunderstood. Some millionaires are killing themselves because they do not have peace, ya'll! This is not a rare phenomenon. We will all experience tribulation. God's Word says, think it not strange concerning the fiery thing that will happen to you. He warns us, and if you are warned, you need to take heed! Seek out the spiritual revelation and plug into God. Receive the spiritual blessing that He wants to give you. He wouldn't have been able to provide you with that spiritual blessing unless you experienced spiritual warfare in the first place. **Many of the challenges that we experience are an opportunity for God to show His mighty hand in our lives. How would you like to see God's mighty hand work in your life?**

BOLDNESS AND COURAGE: WISDOM, KNOWLEDGE, AND UNDERSTANDING

To be bold and courageous requires us to stand on the truth of God's Word and have wisdom, knowledge, and understanding. Why is it easier for us to believe the lies of the negative beliefs? This is because if you believe something, it will seem true. I've stated this before. Many of the thoughts that we have are constantly rehearsed to the point that we begin to develop evidence to affirm the LIE. The enemy wants us to maintain a mindset that is grounded in lies and false beliefs. Why wouldn't he want us to know that God is real? He wants us to be atheists or experience temporary atheism even as self-proclaimed Christians. He wants us to be disconnected from God and be lukewarm about our relationship with God. He doesn't want us to be radical for God.

Nevertheless, God's Word says having wisdom brings life. You all, I need wisdom because I need life. I want to live the life that God has meant and designed for me to live. If I live absent of wisdom, knowledge, and understanding, I'm navigating life foolishly. A fool's ways are wise in his own eyes (Proverbs 12:15). Imagine being ignorant. Have you ever heard of the saying that ignorance is bliss? Ignorance is not bliss. Sure, it was bliss before Adam and Eve ate the forbidden fruit. However, now you need to know what is false and what is true. Now the enemy wants to use ignorance to keep you down and in pain instead of being planted in the truth that gets you on the path of your purpose and answering God's call. Some of us cringe or are upset at being called ignorant or incompetent. However, it doesn't matter how long you've had an ignorant pattern or have lived in sin.

The point of your power is in the present moment! Your power is not stuck in the past. "I wish I could have done this, or I shouldn't have done this" is only another way of saying that I wish I could change the past. Well, we can't do that. We can only focus and change the future. But to change the future, you must change what you focus on today by gathering new information and applying it to your life. It is not the mistakes that you've made that keep you stagnant. Nor is it the negative experiences that you've endured that keep you stagnant. It's the lies that you've been telling yourself that create stagnation! However, in John 8:32, Jesus said, "You shall know the truth, and the truth shall make you free!" Let's do an exercise. Think of your favorite fictional movie or story. Mine was Lion King. When I tell you I've watched Lion King close to 50 or 60 times, it is no exaggeration. I can recite most of the phrases and songs even to this day. Why do you want us to think about our favorite fictional movie or story, Miriam?

Because the lies that you have been telling yourself about your low self-worth and lack of value are no different from a story based on fiction. The fictional story simply is not true! The negative belief that you've been telling yourself is not valid. God can break every chain impacting you! Also, God can rescind every generational curse that has been impacting your family. My motto is that it is your responsibility to define your DNA. What does this mean? This involves diving into God, **neutralizing** your negative beliefs, and **activating** new behaviors based on His Word.

Remember, God is not a man that He should lie nor the man that He needs to repent. With God, you can dominate, create and thrive! God instructs us to be bold and courageous! It takes **courage** to change directions. I've heard the saying when you know better, you do better. This isn't always true. Many of us know that we shouldn't eat chocolate cake at 10 p.m. Many of us know that we don't need to supersize the French fries to be extra extra extra large. Many of us know that high blood pressure affects the black community. However, knowing isn't enough. Having the courage to do something new is a part of creating change. Have courage, my brothers and sisters! Ask God for wisdom, and He will give it to you (James 1:5). Seek it like you're seeking a treasure, and you will find it.

INSECURITY VERSUS GOD'S SPIRIT

Are you feeling empowered? God speaks to you. Intuition is the Holy Spirit inside of you. Many times we condition ourselves to ignore our intuition due to internalizing other people's opinions or seeing ourselves in a way that other people see us and not how God sees us. The enemy plants insecurity. Insecurity is antagonistic toward your intuition. The enemy does not want you to hear God's voice. Again, the enemy is the author of lies. The enemy comes to steal, kill and destroy. God comes that you may have life and have it more abundantly. I can't say that enough.

Many times we have a challenge understanding or discerning between our insecurities and God's Spirit in us. Insecurities will lead you to question who you are. Insecurity encompasses having negative core beliefs about yourself. These beliefs may sound like "I am not good enough, I'm not smart enough, I'm not pretty enough, I'm not handsome enough, I'm not articulate enough, I have never done that before, so I can't, or this is too hard for me." We can be very sophisticated in the way we place limits on ourselves, to the point that we don't see how detrimental those negative beliefs are. Our excuses sound savvy!.

Nevertheless, they are not helpful to your empowerment. On the other hand, God's Spirit inside of you is an internal GPS. It's your God processing system that helps guide your path. It doesn't mean that there won't be a diversion at times. We are imperfect. We can become distracted at times.

God's Holy Spirit is the correction that we need to get back on course. God's Spirit will protect you from going into a dangerous situation. Insecurity will put you in one. Insecurity will use fear to keep you from being empowered. God's Spirit will give you creative ideas for your purpose, and insecurities will lead you to feel that you are not good enough. God's Spirit will empower you to have healthy boundaries, and insecurity will negate the importance of healthy boundaries. God's Spirit allows us to be authentic, truthful, and transparent in our relationships. It will enable us to address issues as they arise, so we can maintain peace. God's Spirit allows us to release relationships that are not healthy because you're developing a growth mindset. Insecurity leads you to perpetuate and maintain toxic relationships for the sake of having them there. **Are you beginning to see the difference?** God's Spirit empowers you, and insecurity disempowers you.

DISCERNMENT

Many of us are wondering whether or not we can trust ourselves to make good choices, especially when we've had a pattern of impaired decision-making. Nevertheless, learning to trust yourself is actually learning to trust God. God is with you. Life is about learning, but this does not mean making decisions in the absence of wisdom, knowledge, and understanding. This means to seek out spiritual revelation and wisdom while you're also making decisions. Plans are successful in the multitude of counselors (Proverbs 15:22).

Developing discernment also requires that you reach out for help and support. Elijah and Elijah was an excellent example of this. They had a godly mentor-mentee relationship. Many times, we need support to reach our goals! This doesn't mean that you can't be independent and autonomous. This means that in order to be a leader, you must be willing to follow and serve. This also necessitates the importance of praying for God to lead you into the appropriate places so that the influence is godly and not just any type of influence.

Many individuals seem to be accelerating in life, but they are not living a godly lifestyle. They are promoting these glamorous ways of being that encompass immorality. As a result, they are in divination with God. Everyone that seems to be accelerating is not for you. Pray for discernment to lead you to a mentor or community that promotes the truth of God and His Word.

Additionally, strengthening your discernment is deciding to be truthful and transparent. Many times we are focused on detecting the liars in our circles, not realizing that we are telling ourselves lies. Any time you have a negative belief about your identity, you are lying to yourself. How can you have mental clarity if your mind or mental capacity is full of false ideas and lies? You must decide to stand on the truth and expose every single lie. Pray for mental clarity. Pray for truth in your life. Remember, the truth shall set you free. The lies shall no longer hold you captive! **What lies do you want to expose? What truth do you want to invite in?**

MAXIMUM WATTAGE OF BOLDNESS AND COURAGE

God's Word says He wants you to be holy for Him. He means that He wants your whole self and not half of you. Imagine dividing a part of you and giving it to God and saying, Lord, I'm going to keep the rest. This will not work, sis or bro. Nor will you survive cutting yourself in half. However, we are doing this in some shape or form if we're not giving ourselves entirely to God. Again God's Word declares that we should be hot or cold and not lukewarm.

Being lukewarm will lead Him to want to spit you out of His mouth. Yuck. Imagine spitting something out. It is so distasteful to God that

that is how He describes the behavior of someone who is a hypocrite or who is double-minded. Think of times when you have been hypocritical or seen hypocrisy happening. This happens in and outside of the church. Unfortunately, when it occurs in the church, it reflects negatively upon the authentic experience of Christianity. Even Moses wasn't allowed to go into the promised land because leadership is supposed to be an example of truth and obedience to God.

Nevertheless, it is up to the people to have an upright walk and relationship with God. Remember, King Saul had favor with God at first, but became double-minded. He began to shift away from God's calling on his life and what God wanted him to do. He cared more about maintaining the popular vote. God's Word says that He grieved even putting Saul in place and had him removed. He replaced him with David, who was the mentee! Do not despise small beginnings.

God will remove big players who are not playing for Him and replace them with those who are meek and humble and in a lower position. God will elevate them to a higher status. When God gives you a position and the crown, protect it by staying in his will! His word says, "I am coming soon. Hold on to what you have, so that no one will take your crown" (Revelation 3:11). Don't let the crown that God has given you be taken by double mindedness! Ask yourself, "Does what I want to do please God or please people? What are my motives?" These are the essential questions that wisdom, knowledge, and understanding prompt you to ask yourself. These are the questions that keep you connected to God as well. I want to do everything I do for God to bring God's glory to it. When I trust that God will take care of me, I don't have to overthink where He is taking me or how I'm going to get there. And when I begin to overthink, I have to remind myself that God has a plan, which allows me to calm down the loud thoughts in my mind so that my spirit can be calm and I can experience His peace.

BE THE LION GOD HAS CALLED YOU TO BE!

God's Word says that the evil people flee when no man comes for them, but the righteous are bold as a lion. If you want to prosper, you must agree with yourself that you are going to be the Lion of Judah. The Lion of Judah is inside of you, and you're going to unleash the impact that the Lion of Judah must release. Many of us have the Lion of Judah inside of us, but we have allowed insecurities and fear to overshadow the lion that is waiting to Roar and come out. Our society is filled with atheists and agnostics who are increasingly displaying and promoting their lack of belief. Yet, many of us as believers can be quite fearful of declaring our belief in God for the sake of assimilation or avoiding persecution. Well, the narrow gate will keep you straight!

THE NARROW GATE

(Luke 13:22-30)
13 Enter in through the narrow gate, for wide the gate and broad the way that leads to destruction, and many enter through it. 14 For narrowed the gate and straightened the path that leads to life, and there are few who find it.

That gate is narrow! The broad way represents "fitting in with society, denying God, and denying your purpose, which leads to utter destruction." I knew a woman who dealt with people-pleasing behavior. This led her to waiver in between what people thought of her and what God said about her. She found herself with a mix of friends. Ones that were atheist and agnostic, and others that were Christian. She had been trying to fit in and relate to non-believers.

The non-believers constantly tormented her; although they did this jokingly, she was offended on the inside. They engaged in illegal activity, violating the boundaries that she had set for herself. When she would hang out or engage in Christian fellowship, she didn't enjoy it. Ultimately, she felt unhappy and exhausted with both groups of people. It wasn't that either group was draining per se. It was that she was creating fatigue within herself by being everything other than her authentic self in Christ. This created a double-minded atmosphere. She was annoyed by other people's fakeness, not realizing that she was being fake herself. She honestly just wanted to belong and not feel lonely. This led me to think about how Jesus would spend time with transgressors and sinners, not just those who were righteous. The Pharisees, of course, questioned Him about it. He responded that if you were well, why would you need a physician? I believe that the difference between Jesus and the scenario above is not about being motivated by just being friendly and not judgmental. Instead, Jesus was motivated by calling all people to repentance. Jesus cared about their redemption and salvation. Jesus didn't hang with them to fit into their lifestyle. He didn't need to censor or filter His belief due to their uncomfortability with truth. He stood on the reality of what He believed so that all humankind could be called to repentance. The gate is narrow. There is no room for you to be double-minded.

Here's a helpful graph that I created to show how "empathy" can lead you in the absence of God's law and healthy boundaries:

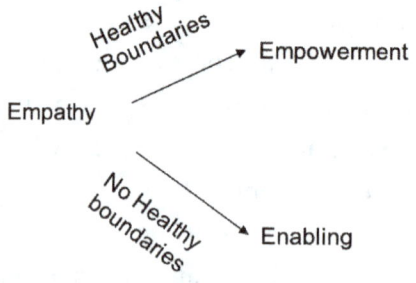

Many of us care and have empathy. God made us loving and caring. However, empathy can either lead towards empowerment or enabling if we're not following God's instruction. The Word of God says obedience is better than sacrifice (1 Samuel 15:22). God's forgiveness is so incredible. His love is unconditional and never fails us.

Nevertheless, have standards. Resist the temptation. **James 4:7 So humble yourselves before God. Resist the devil, and he will flee from you!** Not resisting temptation just because you can be forgiven is not wise. Nor is hanging around with individuals at the sacrifice of your soul. In combination with being obedient to God's Word and Law, empathy leads to protecting your relationship with Him and empowering others to get to know Christ. Empathy in the absence of following God's principles can lead to enabling your sinful nature, as well as theirs if you're going along to get along.

Our society is now placing a major focus on inclusiveness. This is important as prejudices, racism, and hate crimes are beyond problematic. Nevertheless, I've noticed an attack on God's Word, and the removal of it in various organizations, such as school. Be aware of this attack. Be careful not to regard inclusivity as rejecting biblical truth and principles to make others feel comfortable. Believing in God is about standing on the truth of the Word of God and not just falling into the monotonous tradition of going to church and then living the lifestyle of your choosing. It's about living for God 24/7. Look at the following passage:

21 Not everyone who says to me, Lord, Lord, shall enter into the kingdom of the heavens, but he does the will of my Father who is in the heavens. **22** Many shall say to me in that day, Lord, Lord, have we not prophesied through *thy* name, and through *thy* name cast out demons, and through *thy* name done many works of power? **23** and then will I avow unto them, I never knew you. Depart from me, workers of lawlessness. If you don't stand for something, you'll fall for anything. Stand up for God, and He'll stand up for you.

CHAPTER 7

I'M ABOUT MY FATHER'S BUSINESS

"God does business, with those you mean business!" — Adrian Rogers

THE AUDIENCE OF ONE

I once heard this quote "That other people's opinions of you are none of your business."-Lisa Nichols. This is so true. Imagine if Jesus allowed the Pharisees and Sadducees to disrupt how He felt about His purpose and calling. He would have been so distracted, disgruntled, and discouraged. Nevertheless, Jesus stayed focused on God's plan instead of the enemy's plan to disrupt him and distract him. Again, being about your Father's business means focusing on God alone.

One time, while being in my purpose, I made a Facebook post about Daniel trusting God in the lion's den. It specifically stated, "If Daniel can trust God in the Lion's Den, you can trust God with your stress and worries." I posted it and multiple Facebook groups that were Christian-oriented but intentionally decided to post it in one that was not. However, the content was encouraging to many. However, one person commented with hateful speech.

In applying the same concept, other people's opinions about me are none of my business. If I were to have focused on her opinion and hateful rhetoric and become preoccupied with her nasty public message, it could stop me from living my purpose. Our pride and ego don't want to face rejection. However, God hates pride, as it is self-serving and not God-serving. If led by our ego, we would like to defend ourselves in a way that can either show up as fighting the wrong way or hiding. Either way creates discouragement and distraction.

Did I stop posting in the Facebook group? No! I continued to post. My purpose in God is more significant than any negative public opinion! Remember that God is your ultimate defender and vindicator. God wants you to keep your heart open so that you are focused on the task at hand. I prayed for her instead of "fighting back with words." I did not want to misrepresent God in that instance. I could have quickly gone there, and my mind wanted to go, "Who does she think she is? How dare she?" Yet, Jesus experienced the same persecution, and if Jesus experienced it, who am I to think that I won't?

Talking to God about it allowed me to have peace with it. I asked God to cancel every attack spoken from her mouth and asked God to deal with her and the enemy behind it. The enemy was using her at that moment. Know who is behind the attack. I'm not going to have banter with the enemy. I choose to put on the armor of God and pray about it. This can happen with strangers, friends, co-workers, and family!

Many of the enemies' attacks do not seem evident at first. Despite this, staying on guard means protecting your connection with God through constant prayer. STAND VERSUS FALL. If you don't stand for God and the truth of His Word, you can fall for anything. Again, I refer to Adam and Eve as an example. Their responsibility was to guard their purpose and connection with God by not allowing the enemy to manipulate them and not believing the enemy's lies. However, because they were not on guard, their spiritual defenses were porous and weak. Know that the enemy wants to distract you and lead you to be consumed by futile missions. **You must keep on the spiritual armor of God!**

OFFER YOUR BODY AS A LIVING SACRIFICE.

Imagine what would happen if you constantly say yes to God! God used anyone who said yes in mighty and miraculous ways! Let's look at David, for instance. David was a "shepherd boy" who looked after sheep. Goliath and the Philistines were harassing his people. Due to fear, no one wanted to fight Goliath. However, David stood on the truth of God, instead of the opinions of others. It was the people close to him who told him, "You're too small," "you're just a shepherd boy," "You're going to die," etc. Perhaps this was "out of love" due to fear for his life. However, it may be hard for any of us to wrap our minds around our purpose being greater than self-preservation. If you're not living in your purpose, you are not LIVING. There won't be satisfaction in your life because something more significant is calling your name. Ignoring it leads you to futile missions, which is where the enemy wants you to be positioned. David was all in. He was ready to fight for God. He decided that he'd rather live for God than exist in fear, mediocrity, or complacency!

One of my most favorite biblical characters is Deborah, who was a prophet and judge. She heard from God as a prophet, and many individuals would line up to receive her counsel. She operated under the instruction of God. She was known for her courage and actions, which allowed her to live her purpose. Can a woman lead, minister, or pastor? Yes, yes, and yes! She didn't look at her gender as a barrier. Sure others may have done so. However, God appoints us to do His work. Not only was she a Judge and Prophet, but she also ministered and advised the leader of an army of 10,000 plus soldiers! From the words of Susan Nelson, "If God is telling you to do something or go somewhere, despite your fears, listen to His call. He has plans that we cannot begin to understand, and our obedience may change hearts and lives." The old saying **"God doesn't call the qualified, He qualifies the called"** applies here. Doing something out of your comfort zone to glorify Him can be terrifying, but faith was never promised to be easy. Be bold. Be courageous - for His glory. Never waver in your faith. We may not always know what the road ahead will look like, but we only need to remember that God will faithfully guide us and lead the way.

You were bought with a price. Your body is the Temple of the Holy Spirit. You are not your own. Knowing who you are is not going to be accomplished unless you know who you belong to. You are a child of the Most High God!

BE PURPOSE-DRIVEN!

We're too busy living lives of performance that we don't know who we are in Christ. We've become performance-driven instead of purpose-driven. However, when I give up doing something my way and am led by God, I will find myself and my purpose. I will find myself because my identity is in Him. I leave the performance, and I step into purpose. God is calling you to take the performance-driven/ people-pleasing mask off! You are original. You are unique, and you are peculiar. You are made in His Image. Get off of social media and stop comparing yourself to the next person! Your journey is your business and God's business! God's Word says not just in my presence but also in my absence, handle your salvation with fear and trembling (Philippians 2:12). Guarding and activating your purpose is your responsibility.

Love what God loves and hate what God hates. Suppose you invite God into your living room. Would He love what you're watching? If He were listening to your radio, would He love what you're listening to? This content is not "too spiritual." Philippians 4:8 says to think on pure things and of good report, think of lovely and honest things. These things are our thoughts. This is your filter. When I Immerse myself into the ways of God, I commit to cleansing myself from all filthiness of the flesh so I can perfect Holiness in the fear of God. Why would we pollute our minds and position ourselves with the principalities of this world? Make a declaration like this one: "The company I keep will be equally yoked, Lord. I will not position myself to be in divination. Those I surround myself with will be people who want to be spiritually rich in you God. I will surround myself with people who hunger and thirst for you!"

The principles of God are simple. However, the ways of the righteous require much endurance, love, hope, peace, long-suffering goodness and meekness. In our human capacity, we understand simplicity but have tried to oversimplify the process as a matter of convenience. There is no Google download for patience. There is no Google download for perseverance and bouncing back from setbacks. There is no Google download for purpose and peace. We've been so set on playing it safe and being self-preserving and led by foolishness and ignorance. We do not realize that insanity and foolishness come with a cost. We've become sophisticated in our degrees, but there's a scarcity of love, purpose, and peace. There's a rarity in knowing who we are in God. There's a cost, and it's a bill bigger than Sallie Mae. It comes at the expense of not fulfilling your God-given purpose. Many of us think that failure is fatal, but not living up to your goal is the real tragedy. Jesus says, come as you are!

BE UNIQUELY YOU, DREAM AND CREATE

Child of God, you are peculiar and unique. When I think of this concept, I again think of Joseph. Joseph was a dreamer, just like you. You have ideas, visions, and dreams that you would like to pursue. Perhaps you shared them with somebody, and they laughed at you. Maybe you are looking at yourself through somebody else's lens. Perhaps you've done it for so long that it's hard for you to feel motivated even to pursue your dreams. Perhaps you think that you would fail if you tried anyway. Well, I came to tell you that you have an impact within you that is so great that only God knows it and can help you with it. God understands and is all knowledgeable. People, even the ones closest to you, are not meant to understand.

Let's look at Joseph once more. Joseph was highly favored by his father, Jacob. Joseph had 12 or so other brothers who were jealous of him and the favoritism shown to him. Joseph had a dream, and he was shown to be a leader to whom they would bow down. They did not like this. They were so jealous and would covet their brother that they plotted against him. Joseph's dad asked him to go and check on the brothers who were off doing something naughty. When Joseph went out of care and concern, as well as obedience, they grabbed him. They plotted to murder him. However, one of the brothers said not to do it. He came up with a plan to instead sell him into slavery.

Meanwhile, they put him into a ditch- a deep hole in the ground. Joseph could not get out of this ditch himself and would have needed help. However, when they did take him out, instead of taking him back home, they allowed strangers to take him. How horrific is that? His own family, his blood, betrayed him and got rid of him.

Furthermore, they killed an animal, took the coat of many colors that their father gave Joseph, and wiped the blood. They took it home and told their father that an animal had killed Joseph when he was actually sold into slavery. They plotted to kill him. They faked his death and went on about their business. They are the real original gangsters, seriously. The FBI has nothing on them.

However, God is above all and knows all. As I said before, what the enemy plans for evil, God will turn it into something good. As we know, Joseph had God's favor. And when you have God's favor, any scheme of the enemy to make you fall and fail will not work. Joseph was placed in leadership positions because of God's favor.

Nevertheless, the tragedy doesn't end there. Potiphar's wife tried to seduce him. He did not look to the left or right. He made a decisive decision that he was not going to be seduced by her and chose God instead. She falsely accused him of wanting to assault her and was placed in jail for two years. Can you imagine being placed in jail when you did nothing wrong? I know I've heard and seen stories of this happening, and the stories are completely surreal.

Nevertheless, God's favor followed him, even while he was in jail. Joseph could have chosen to remove himself from God's presence. However, he decided to trust God. He didn't have the knowledge or understanding to know what was going to happen next. We often read these Bible stories and hear them so much that you almost believe that the character knows what will happen ahead of time. Joseph didn't know. He trusted God. Then came the Baker and Winemaker from Pharaoh's house, who were put in prison. Joseph interpreted their dreams and asked them to remember him when they returned to Pharaoh's home. Eventually, one of them did and told Pharaoh. Pharaoh had a dream that no one could interpret. Therefore, when the bread maker told Pharaoh about Joseph, Pharaoh asked Joseph to be released and he was placed in an even higher position! Because Joseph decided to stay plugged into God, God used him in a VERY UNIQUE way! **What are your dreams or desires? How does aligning yourself with the Kingdom of God get you closer to your purpose?**

ABIDE IN THE PEACE OF GOD

God uses everything for our good! Les Brown says, "If you fall, fall on your back because if you can look up, you can get up." And I say, "When you're in the ditch, all you can do is look up. Look up to the hills from where your help comes from!" How do we get out of the ditch? Many times the ditch feels like an entrapment. But you are meant to hold your hands up. **Hold your hands up and pray.** Pray for God's direction and allow His divine orchestration and facilitation to lift you out of the ditch and take you to a deeper place in Him. He will elevate you in the process. Being in the ditch leads to a breakthrough and a come-up on the other side! **Are you ready to answer the calling of God on your life?** James 2:26 says, "Faith without works is dead!" Do it now! Do it unprepared and imperfect! Have courage and be bold! Your potential is already inside of you, and God wants to unclog it. He's the master potter, and plumber! Your purpose shall be released in Jesus' mighty name! In a world of so much turmoil, violence, and immorality, there is no time to waste. Don't waste your purpose because of self-preserving behaviors that are guided by your ego. I dare you to take a step, and before you know it, you will be running a good race of courage, towards a higher calling on your life! I pray you and I hear the most validating words one day, "Well done, thy good and faithful servant!"

CONCLUSION

Congratulations on completing this book! If you or anyone you know would like support in deepening their relationship with God, shifting away from people-pleasing behavior, and finding peace and purpose, contact me here: https://define-your-dna.com/. For additional bonuses or information regarding one-to-one therapy or to inquire about my group coaching program also visit, https://define-your-dna.com/. Additionally, if you would like to support and use your platform for a great purpose, take a picture of yourself and this book. Post it on your social media with the hashtag #defineyourDNA and #Ihavepurpose. God bless you!

Prayer to Receive Christ as your Savior:

Jesus, I believe you are the Son of God, that you died on the cross to rescue me from sin and death and to restore me to the Father. I choose now to turn from my sins, my self-centeredness, and every part of my life that does not please you. I choose you. I give myself to you. I receive your forgiveness and ask you to take your rightful place in my life as my Savior and Lord. Come reign in my heart, fill me with your love and your life, and help me to become a person who is truly loving—a person like you. Restore me, Jesus. Live in me. Love through me. Thank you, God. In Jesus' name I pray. Amen.

Prayer of Consecrating Your Body:

I present my body to Jesus Christ as a living sacrifice; I present the members of my body to Jesus Christ as instruments of righteousness. My body has been bought with the blood of Jesus Christ and it belongs to him. My body is a temple of the Holy Spirit. I renounce every way my body has been misused and abused, and every way that I have misused and abused my body; I bring all those acts under the atoning blood of Jesus Christ. I rededicate my body and all its parts to the loving rule of Jesus Christ; I dedicate and consecrate my body to him in every way. I ask for the blood of Christ to cleanse my body and make it holy once more. Holy Spirit, come and fill your temple now; restore my body under the complete dominion of Jesus Christ. Thank you for healing me and making me whole again, in Jesus' name, Amen.

Prayer of Consecrating My Sexuality:

Jesus, I confess here and now that you are my Creator and therefore the Creator of my sexuality. I confess that you are also my Savior, that you have ransomed me with your blood and you are therefore the Savior of my sexuality. I have been bought with the blood of Jesus Christ; my life and my body belong to God; my sexuality belongs to God. Jesus, I present myself to you now to be made whole and holy in every way, including in my sexuality. You ask us to present our bodies to you as living sacrifices and the parts of our bodies as instruments of righteousness. I do this now. I present my body, my sexuality ("as a man" or "as a woman") and I present my sexual nature to you. In Jesus' name, Amen!

ABOUT THE AUTHOR

Miriam Matthews was born and raised in Atlanta, Georgia. During her childhood, she enjoyed being adventurous and exploring the outdoors! She has always been a nurturer and genuinely cares about others. As a child, she experienced various types of trauma, including sexual trauma, but she did not notice its impacts until years later. She faced challenges with insecurities and developed a keen awareness of other people's reactions toward her. She developed associations at a very young age that guided how she would interact with people and the world. Miriam developed Rules of Engagement that influenced her positively and negatively in public and private settings. Miriam created a dichotomy of herself, as she wanted to relate socially as best as possible. The need to fit in became the story of her life. Miriam recognized later that this is an innate part of being human, but this began to rule her in a completely unhealthy and antagonistic way. She attended a church since birth, but her attendance declined when she went to college. We often think of college as a time to find ourselves, but Miriam felt that she became even more lost. The identity loss was already there but became more pronounced.

Nevertheless, something about wanting to help others stuck with her. She was attracted to behavioral health, likely because of her own need for stability. Many times the individuals that face the most opposition, that have the passion and are the best teachers! This was Miriam. She developed a passion for wanting to help others which actually led to her getting the help that she needed. She obtained her bachelor's and Masters of Social Work degrees at Georgia State University. She completed her Graduate Studies in 2013. Miriam reconnected with her high-school sweetheart and they got married shortly after he joined the military in 2016. They moved from Georgia to Massachusetts, where marriage life began. She became pregnant with her second child and now she has two beautiful girls! Miriam found identity in being a mother and wife and realized that God gave her a spouse and girls to love that helped cultivate her! As the years went by, she realized that a fire was burning deep inside of her that wanted to come out. This was her light, but she wasn't comfortable showing it. Miriam felt that she had to keep it "safe," so she would blow it out at times before it could be blown out by somebody else. It was fairly easy to stay hidden where they were, as Miriam wasn't deeply rooted in this state even though they stayed there for a few years.

Nevertheless, when Miriam turned 30 years old, something changed within her. She felt like her state of being was mediocre, and it caused so much frustration within herself that she was going to implode like a volcano. Miriam went through multiple processes in God, of exposing every lie that the enemy had been telling her for years, which allowed her to begin to ground herself in the truth of who God was calling her to be. Miriam invested in her spiritual growth and personal growth! Because of faith and works, God has created a major transformation in her life that is continuing to happen. She now honors her unique anointing, brilliance, and creativity for the Kingdom of God! She realized that her PAST was her PUSH for her PURPOSE! God has placed a passion on her heart to help women stop perpetuating pain and push towards their purpose!

Miriam now has a successful therapy practice and Christian Coaching Business for Professional Christian Women seeking purpose! God has shown His mighty hand in her life, and Miriam is thrilled to share His gospel, her story, and continues to answer His call to go higher in Him!

INDEX

E

I

J

M

www.ingramcontent.com/pod-product-compliance
Lightning Source LLC
Chambersburg PA
CBHW051005140626
46546CB00016B/867